Ember.js Cookbook

Arm yourself with over 65 hands-on recipes to master the
skills of building scalable web applications with Ember.js

Erik Hanchett

[PACKT]
PUBLISHING

open source
community experience distilled

BIRMINGHAM - MUMBAI

Ember.js Cookbook

First published: February 2016

Production reference: 1220216

Published by Packt Publishing Ltd.
Livery Place
35 Livery Street
Birmingham B3 2PB, UK.

ISBN 978-1-78398-220-2

www.packtpub.com

Credits

Author
Erik Hanchett

Reviewer
Zoltan Debre

Commissioning Editor
Amarabha Banerjee

Acquisition Editor
Manish Nainani

Content Development Editor
Preeti Singh

Technical Editor
Suwarna Patil

Copy Editor
Tasneem Fatehi

Project Coordinator
Dinesh Rathe

Proofreader
Safis Editing

Indexer
Monica Ajmera Mehta

Graphics
Disha Haria

Production Coordinator
Conidon Miranda

Cover Work
Conidon Miranda

About the Author

Erik Hanchett is a software developer, blogger, and perpetual student who has been writing code for over 10 years. He currently resides in Reno, Nevada, with his wife and two kids. He blogs about software development at `ProgramWithErik.com`.

I would like to thank my wife, Susan, for helping me stay motivated, my friend, F. B. Wood, for all his help on the English language, and Dr. Bret Simmons for teaching me the value of a personal brand.

I would also like to thank all my friends and family who encouraged me along the way.

About the Reviewer

Zoltan Debre is a lecturer, economist, journalist, and software engineer. He has been building websites and web applications since 1997 for big corporations and small start-ups worldwide in Budapest, Dublin, and recently in Wellington, New Zealand. Furthermore, he is researching at Victoria University of Wellington. As a full stack software engineer, Zoltan uses various tools and languages such as Ruby, JavaScript, Java, PHP, Dart, Lua, and Go. He is an advocate of efficient development tools and frameworks, and for this reason, he is an active supporter of Ruby on Rails and a committed evangelist of Ember.js.

He's been working with Ember.js since 2012, and he follows the evolution of the framework and its influence on the whole JavaScript ecosystem. His mission is to teach and show how quickly developers can deliver a project with a very efficient framework. For this reason, he voluntarily runs workshops and gives presentations, and he teaches Ember.js to junior and senior developers and students. He writes tutorials, shares examples, and tirelessly helps other developers. Follow his work or contact him on www.yoember.com, www.zoltan.nz, and www.emberjs.nz.

www.PacktPub.com

eBooks, discount offers, and more

Did you know that Packt offers eBook versions of every book published, with PDF and ePub files available? You can upgrade to the eBook version at www.PacktPub.com and as a print book customer, you are entitled to a discount on the eBook copy. Get in touch with us at customercare@packtpub.com for more details.

At www.PacktPub.com, you can also read a collection of free technical articles, sign up for a range of free newsletters and receive exclusive discounts and offers on Packt books and eBooks.

https://www2.packtpub.com/books/subscription/packtlib

Do you need instant solutions to your IT questions? PacktLib is Packt's online digital book library. Here, you can search, access, and read Packt's entire library of books.

Why Subscribe?

- ▶ Fully searchable across every book published by Packt
- ▶ Copy and paste, print, and bookmark content
- ▶ On demand and accessible via a web browser

Table of Contents

Preface

Single-page, client-side JavaScript frameworks may possibly be the future of the Web. Client-side frameworks have matured a lot in the last few years. They've made creating web applications easier and more responsive. Ember.js has been one of the leading frameworks behind this movement.

This book provides in-depth explanations of how to use the Ember.js framework to take you from being a beginner to an expert. You'll start with the basics, and by the end of the book, you'll have a solid foundation in creating real-time web applications in Ember.

We'll begin by explaining key points on how to use the Ember.js framework and associated tools. You'll learn how to use Ember CLI effectively and how to create and deploy your application. We'll take a close look at the Ember object model and templates by looking at bindings and observers. We'll move on to Ember components and models and Ember Data. Next, we'll look at testing with integration and acceptance tests using QUnit. Afterward, we'll take a look at authentication and services and working with Ember add-ons. We'll explore advanced topics such as services and initializers and how to use them together to build real-time applications.

What this book covers

Chapter 1, *Ember CLI Basics*, shows you how to use the Ember CLI command-line tool and deal with upgrading and deploying your project.

Chapter 2, *The Ember.Object Model*, demonstrates how to create Ember objects and instances and use bindings, mixins, and enumerables.

Chapter 3, *Ember Templates*, tells you how to use templates and template helpers.

Chapter 4, *Ember Router*, demonstrates how to set up your model and work with loading states and redirection.

Chapter 5, Ember Controllers, explains how to use properties and manage dependencies between controllers.

Chapter 6, Ember Components, covers passing properties, events, and actions.

Chapter 7, Ember Models and Ember Data, explains how to manipulate records and customize adapters.

Chapter 8, Logging, Debugging, and Testing, demonstrates how to create acceptance and unit tests as well as the Ember Inspector.

Chapter 9, Real-Life Tasks with Ember.js, discusses how to use services, authentication, Bootstrap, and Liquid Fire.

Chapter 10, Awesome Tasks with Ember, explains how to use Ember validations, Firebase, WebSockets, and server-side rendering.

Chapter 11, Real-Time Web Applications, discusses how to use dependency injection, application initializers, run loops, and create add-ons.

What you need for this book

- ▶ Windows, Mac OS X, or Linux
- ▶ NPM 2.x or greater
- ▶ Node 4.0 or higher, freely obtained from `http://www.nodejs.org`
- ▶ Bower 1.4 or greater

Who this book is for

Anyone who wants to explore Ember.js and wishes to get hands-on experience making sophisticated web apps with less coding will find this book handy. Prior experience of coding and familiarity with JavaScript is recommended. If you've heard of Ember.js or are just curious on how a single-page application framework works, then this book is for you.

Sections

In this book, you will find several headings that appear frequently (*Getting ready, How to do it..., How it works..., There's more...,* and *See also*).

To give clear instructions on how to complete a recipe, we use these sections as follows:

Getting ready

This section tells you what to expect in the recipe, and describes how to set up any software or any preliminary settings required for the recipe.

How to do it...

This section contains the steps required to follow the recipe.

How it works...

This section usually consists of a detailed explanation of what happened in the previous section.

There's more...

This section consists of additional information about the recipe in order to make the reader more knowledgeable about the recipe.

See also

This section provides helpful links to other useful information for the recipe.

Conventions

In this book, you will find a number of text styles that distinguish between different kinds of information. Here are some examples of these styles and an explanation of their meaning.

Code words in text, database table names, folder names, filenames, file extensions, pathnames, dummy URLs, user input, and Twitter handles are shown as follows: "We can include other contexts through the use of the `include` directive."

A block of code is set as follows:

```
{
  "usePods": true
}
```

When we wish to draw your attention to a particular part of a code block, the relevant lines or items are set in bold:

```
const Light = Ember.Object.extend({
  isOn: false,
  color: 'yellow',
  age: null,
  description: Ember.computed('isOn','color',function() {
    return 'The ' + this.get('color') + ' light is set to '
      + this.get('isOn');
  }),
  fullDescription:
    Ember.computed('description','age',function() {
    return this.get('description') + ' and the age is ' +
      this.get('age')
  }),
  aliasDescription: Ember.computed.alias('fullDescription')
});

const bulb = Light.create({age: 22});
bulb.get('aliasDescription');
  //The yellow light is set to false and the age is 22.
```

Any command-line input or output is written as follows:

```
$ ember server --port 1234
```

New terms and **important words** are shown in bold. Words that you see on the screen, for example, in menus or dialog boxes, appear in the text like this: "The message on the screen will show **Hello World! My name is John Smith. Hello World! My name is Erik Hanchett.**"

 Warnings or important notes appear in a box like this.

 Tips and tricks appear like this.

Reader feedback

Feedback from our readers is always welcome. Let us know what you think about this book—what you liked or disliked. Reader feedback is important for us as it helps us develop titles that you will really get the most out of.

To send us general feedback, simply e-mail feedback@packtpub.com, and mention the book's title in the subject of your message.

If there is a topic that you have expertise in and you are interested in either writing or contributing to a book, see our author guide at www.packtpub.com/authors.

Customer support

Now that you are the proud owner of a Packt book, we have a number of things to help you to get the most from your purchase.

Downloading the example code

You can download the example code files from your account at http://www.packtpub.com for all the Packt Publishing books you have purchased. If you purchased this book elsewhere, you can visit http://www.packtpub.com/support and register to have the files e-mailed directly to you.

Errata

Although we have taken every care to ensure the accuracy of our content, mistakes do happen. If you find a mistake in one of our books—maybe a mistake in the text or the code—we would be grateful if you could report this to us. By doing so, you can save other readers from frustration and help us improve subsequent versions of this book. If you find any errata, please report them by visiting http://www.packtpub.com/submit-errata, selecting your book, clicking on the **Errata Submission Form** link, and entering the details of your errata. Once your errata are verified, your submission will be accepted and the errata will be uploaded to our website or added to any list of existing errata under the Errata section of that title.

To view the previously submitted errata, go to https://www.packtpub.com/books/content/support and enter the name of the book in the search field. The required information will appear under the **Errata** section.

Piracy

Piracy of copyrighted material on the Internet is an ongoing problem across all media. At Packt, we take the protection of our copyright and licenses very seriously. If you come across any illegal copies of our works in any form on the Internet, please provide us with the location address or website name immediately so that we can pursue a remedy.

Please contact us at copyright@packtpub.com with a link to the suspected pirated material.

We appreciate your help in protecting our authors and our ability to bring you valuable content.

Questions

If you have a problem with any aspect of this book, you can contact us at questions@packtpub.com, and we will do our best to address the problem.

Ember CLI Basics

1

In this chapter, we will cover the following recipes:

- ► Installing Ember CLI
- ► Creating your first project
- ► Exploring pods and the folder layout
- ► Asset compilation
- ► Dependency management
- ► Upgrading your project
- ► Deployment

Introduction

Ember CLI is a **Node.js**-based command-line interface tool designed for application programming in **Ember.js**. Since its creation, this tool has become the preferred method to create Ember applications.

Simply put, Ember CLI makes starting a new Ember application easy. In other frameworks, you might need to learn **gulp** or **grunt** as your task runners. In Ember CLI, this is all built-in for you. Having Ember CLI in the Ember.js ecosystem is a game changer and makes this framework stand out above the rest.

Ember CLI handles testing, compiling, and upgrading, and even has a built-in web server. Ember CLI not only generates boilerplate code for you, but it also integrates nicely with many testing frameworks. It has a robust add-on system that extends the functionality well beyond its current capabilities.

Installing Ember CLI

The installation of Ember CLI is essential to learning Ember and will be used throughout this book.

Getting ready

Before the installation of Ember CLI, we must have the **Node Package Manager** (**npm**) installed. npm is a package manager for JavaScript and is installed by default with Node.js.

You must install version 0.12 or later of Node.js for Ember CLI to run. If you can, try to install version 4.0.0 or higher. This is the preferred version.

Node.js is available in several major platforms including Windows, Mac, and Linux. There are several ways to install Node.js:

- ▶ **One-click installers**: Many platforms such as Windows and Mac have this available
- ▶ **Homebrew** or **MacPorts**: This is useful for Mac OS users
- ▶ **Download TAR file**: Download a TAR file of Node.js and extract
- ▶ **Install via the Linux package management system**: Yum, apt-get, or pacman can be used to install on a Linux environment

A one-click installer for Windows or Mac

This method is by far the easiest. To install node, you'll need to open the node website at http://nodejs.org/download. Click on the pkg, msi, or exe installer for Windows or Mac. Run it after it's downloaded.

Homebrew or MacPorts for Mac

If you already have Homebrew installed, just run the following command:

```
$ brew install node
```

On the other hand, if you are running MacPorts, you can use the port install command:

```
$ sudo port install nodejs
```

> MacPorts can be installed from http://www.macports.org. Homewbrew can be installed from http://brew.sh. Both offer simple package management for OS X systems.

A TAR file

A TAR file is a type of archive file. To install node via a TAR, you will need to download the TAR file from the Node.js website and extract and install it. One way of doing this is to use `curl`.

I would only recommend this method if you are using a Linux distribution. If you are running on Linux, you'll need the right tools installed to compile from source. On Ubuntu, you'll need to install the build-essential and `curl` packages:

```
$ curl http://nodejs.org/dist/node-latest.tar.gz | tar xz --strip-
components=1
$ ./configure
$ sudo make install
```

The Linux package manager

All major Linux distributions offer Node.js packages. In Ubuntu, you can simply use `apt-get`:

```
$ sudo apt-get install nodejs
```

In Fedora, you can use `yum`:

```
$ yum install nodejs npm
```

Check with your Linux distribution to find out more details on how to install packages such as Node.js. Be aware that some distributions might offer outdated versions of Node.js. In this case, I would recommend that you use the **Node Version Manager** (**NVM**) installation method that will be discussed later.

Test installation

To test your installation, run the `-v` command:

```
$ node -v
$ npm -v
```

This will show the current installed version. Keep in mind that you must run v0.12 or above to run Ember CLI. If possible, try to run v4.0.0 or above.

 The NVM is a bash script that helps manage multiple active Node.js versions. NVM offers a very simple command-line interface to install any version of Node.js without having to visit the Node.js website. It separates each installation making it very easy to change between versions. I would recommend most beginners on Mac and Linux to run this. You can download NVM at `https://github.com/creationix/nvm`.

How to do it...

We'll need to use `npm` to install Ember CLI. We'll install it globally with the `-g` option so that it can be run anywhere from the command line.

1. Open the command prompt and type the following command:

    ```
    $ sudo npm install -g ember-cli
    ```

    If NVM was installed, you don't need `sudo` at the start of the command.

2. After Ember CLI is installed, we'll need to download **Bower**. Bower is a package manager for client-side programming and another essential component of Ember.js. Node.js and npm must be installed before beginning the installation of Bower. We'll be using Bower to install all our client-side libraries:

    ```
    $ sudo npm install -g bower
    ```

    Similar to the last command, you don't need `sudo` at the start of the command if Node.js was installed via NVM.

3. The last step is to install **PhantomJS**. PhantomJS is a scripted headless browser used to automate and test web pages. It's preferred by Ember CLI and needs to be installed:

    ```
    $ npm install -g phantomjs
    ```

4. If you are on Windows, install the Ember CLI Windows tool:

    ```
    $ npm install ember-cli-windows -g
    ```

5. Once installed, this tool can be run in any project directory:

    ```
    $ ember-cli-windows
    ```

6. Make sure to download and install Git for Windows: `https://git-scm.com/downloads`

Working with Windows

Build times on Windows can be longer then Mac or Linux. The Ember CLI Windows tool can help speed up and optimize build performance. Just run it in the project directory. You can also download it as an add-on instead.

Another way to help with performance is to always run PowerShell/CMD with elevated privileges. Otherwise, performance issues and errors might occur. Lastly, try to use npm version 3 or higher. You may run into issues with long file paths with older versions in Windows.

Another handy tip is as follows:

Optional: Install Watchman

Watchman is a file-watching service for OS X and UNIX-like operating systems. It was developed by Facebook and is a more effective way for Ember CLI to watch project changes. If it's not installed, Ember CLI will fall back to using **NodeWatcher**. NodeWatcher is more error-prone and has trouble observing large trees. Install Watchman if your platform supports it. To download and configure Watchman, visit `https://facebook.github.io/watchman/`.

How it works...

Ember CLI is written in Node.js and can be installed via npm. The tool interprets commands from the user to help create an Ember.js application. Each command from the user is looked up and then executed. Ember CLI relies on several other dependencies including Bower, Lodash, Broccoli, and Babel, to name a few.

There's more...

Let's take a look at commands and aliases.

Commands

Once Ember CLI is installed, we'll have access to several commands. Here is a short list of some of the more important ones:

Command	Purpose
`ember`	This prints a list of available commands
`ember new <name-of-app>`	This creates a directory called `<name-of-app>` and creates the application structure
`ember init`	This creates an application in the current directory
`ember build`	This builds the application in the `/dist` folder
`ember server`	This starts a web server
`ember generate <generator-name>`	This runs a generator that builds scaffolding for the project
`ember destroy <generator-name>`	This uninstalls the module that was created by the generator
`ember test`	This runs tests using **Testem**
`ember install <addon-name>`	This installs add-ons

Aliases

Keep in mind that for every command, there is an alias. These aliases make it a little quicker to run commands. Suppose that you wanted to build a new project. Normally, you would type this:

```
$ ember build
```

This will work and is fine. It will generate a new project and application structure. You can also use an alias.

```
$ ember b
```

Here is a list of some common aliases that you can use. This is optional.

Command	Alias
ember build	ember b
ember generate	ember g
ember init	ember i
ember server	ember s
ember destroy	ember d
ember test	ember t
ember version	ember v

Creating your first project

In this recipe we'll create our first project.

How to do it...

We'll begin with the Ember CLI tool to create our first project.

1. Open the command prompt and type the following command:

    ```
    $ ember new my-project
    ```

    This will create a brand new project called my-project. The project structure will have everything that we need to get started.

2. To display this project, we can simply run the server command:

```
$ cd my-project
$ ember server
```

The `ember server` command will start up a web server on port 4200. You can access this port by opening `http://localhost:4200`. You should see the default **Welcome to Ember website**.

> It is a good idea to keep the Ember server running while developing your application. Ember CLI uses a tool called **LiveReload** to refresh the web browser when changes are made. This can be useful to see how new changes are affecting your application. To run LiveReload, simply type `ember server`. This will start the server with LiveReload.

3. The server command defaults to port 4200. You can easily change this using the `--port` argument:

```
$ ember server --port 1234
```

This will start the server on port `1234` instead of the default 4200.

4. Another useful option is the `--proxy` argument. This will proxy all **Asynchronous JavaScript and XML (Ajax)** requests to the given address. Let's say that we have a node server running on port `8080`. We can run the server as follows:

```
$ ember server --proxy http://127.0.0.1:8080
```

For every Ajax request, Ember now will send these requests to the localhost at port `8080`.

> Keep in mind that as of Ember 2.0, **Internet Explorer (IE)** 8 support has been dropped. All modern web browsers and versions of IE after 8 work fine. If by chance IE 8 support is needed, Ember.js version 1.13 has extended browser support and should work with it.

How it works...

The `ember server` command creates a **Node.js Express server**. This server uses LiveReload and refreshes the web page whenever any changes are made. The server command accepts different arguments, including `--proxy` and `--port`.

There's more...

When running the server, you have access to tests. After you start the server, you'll have access to the **QUnit** interface. QUnit is a JavaScript unit testing framework. It is used to run your integration and acceptance tests. To access the interface, navigate your browser to `http://localhost:4200/tests`. This will show all your tests in the project. From here, you can see which tests passed and which failed. We will cover this in the later chapters:

MyNewApp Tests

☐ Hide passed tests ☐ Check for Globals ☐ No try-catch ☐ Hide container

QUnit 1.20.0; Mozilla/5.0 (Windows NT 10.0; WOW64) AppleWebKit/537.36 (KHT

Tests completed in 307 milliseconds.
23 assertions of 23 passed, 0 failed.

1. JSHint - .: app.js should pass jshint (1)

2. JSHint - components/my-component: components/my-component/component

3. JSHint - hello: hello/controller.js should pass jshint (1)

4. JSHint - hello: hello/route.js should pass jshint (1)

Exploring pods and the folder layout

Ember CLI will create our folder structure for us. Ember.js uses the **model-view-controller** (**MVC**) pattern. You'll see in this recipe how the folder structure is laid out and how the model, controller, and view (templates) are separated from each other.

Getting ready

Ember CLI relies on **ES2015** modules. This means that you can write code today using tomorrow's JavaScript syntax. This is accomplished via the **Ember Resolver**.

ES2015

ECMAScript 6, also known as ES2015, is the upcoming version of the ECMAScript programming language. ES2015 includes several new features, including template strings, destructuring, arrow functions, modules, and class definitions, to name a few. This is all available now within your Ember project.

Pods

An ember pod is a different type of structure that organizes your modules by feature instead of type. As your project grows, you may want to organize your project by feature to help keep things organized. The Ember Resolver will look for a pod structure first before it looks at the traditional structure.

To set up the pod structure automatically, you can edit the .ember-cli file in the root of your project directory and add this line:

```
{
  "usePods": true
}
```

Downloading the example code

You can download the example code files from your account at http://www.packtpub.com for all the Packt Publishing books you have purchased. If you purchased this book elsewhere, you can visit http://www.packtpub.com/support and register to have the files e-mailed directly to you.

This will set the default structure to always use pods. When using pods, it is a good idea to set the location where all pods live. To do this, you will need to edit the config/environment.js file:

```
...
var ENV = {
  modulePrefix: 'pod-example',

..    podModulePrefix: 'pod-example/pods'
```

The podModulePrefix property sets the POD path with the following format, {appname}/{poddir}. In the preceding example, the pod directory is now set to /pods in the app folder. If the location is not set, all new modules will be created in the app/ folder.

How to do it...

After a new project is created, a normal folder layout is generated. This layout consists of several different types of modules. Here is a short description of each directory:

Directory	What it does
app/adapters	Adapters help extend logic to communicate with a backend data store
app/components	Components are used to help reuse code and must have a dash in their name

Directory	What it does
app/helpers	Helpers are used for HTML reuse
app/initializers	Initializers are run first and help set up your application
app/mixins	This is a special type of **Ember.Object** used with multiple inheritance
app/routes	Routes help move through different application states
app/serializers	This serializes your data model
app/transform	Transform is used to deserialize and serialize model attributes
app/utils	Utils are small utility classes
app/models	Models hold the data store
app/templates	Templates use HTMLBars to display HTML to the user
app/templates/components	These are templates used in your components

A new project app folder with a default layout will look similar to this:

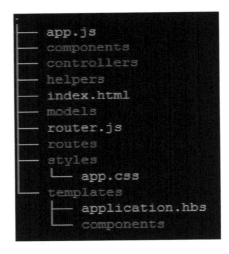

Each module will have its own directory. For example, the templates folder will store all the templates while the components controller will store all the components.

Let's say that we added a new post resource using pods. The following command will generate a new post model, route, and template, and it will update the router:

```
$ ember g resource posts
```

Now the filesystem will look like this:

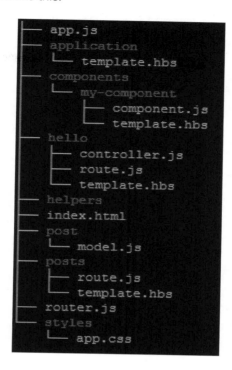

```
├── app.js
├── application
│   └── template.hbs
├── components
│   └── my-component
│       ├── component.js
│       └── template.hbs
├── hello
│   ├── controller.js
│   ├── route.js
│   └── template.hbs
├── helpers
├── index.html
├── post
│   └── model.js
├── posts
│   ├── route.js
│   └── template.hbs
├── router.js
└── styles
    └── app.css
```

Pods sorts directories by features. The post and posts folders are features and the files are named after the function they serve.

How it works...

The directory structure in each Ember CLI project is by design. When creating a new project or generating new scaffolding, the CLI will place files in a certain directory with a certain naming structure that the Ember Resolver understands using the ES2015 format.

The Ember Resolver is responsible for the looking up of code in your application and converting the name conventions in the actual class files. With Ember pods, the resolver knows to look there first before the default structure.

Asset compilation

In this recipe we'll take a look at how assets are added to a project.

How to do it...

In your application, at some point, you may want to add assets and minimize or fingerprint your project. This is done in the `root` folder of your project in the `ember-cli-build.js` file or in the `asset` folder.

CSS and assets

All the assets should be placed in the `public/assets` folder. The assets can be referred throughout the program at `assets/images/{image file}`. CSS files should be placed in the `app/styles` folder.

Minifying

By default, CSS and JavaScript files are minified during the production build process. There are ways to turn this functionality on and off. For example, let's say that you want to turn off the minification for both CSS and JavaScript. To do this, we can simply edit the `ember-cli-build.js` file, and under the `// Add options here` section, add the `minifyCSS` and `minifyJS` section:

```
module.exports = function(defaults) {
  var app = new EmberApp(defaults, {
    // Add options here
    minifyCSS: {
      enabled: false
    },
    minifyJS: {
      enabled: false
    }
  });
```

This will tell the compiler not to minify JavaScript and CSS. To build the application in the production mode, simply use the `--environment` argument:

```
$ ember build --enviroment=production
```

Fingerprinting

All files by default will be fingerprinted during the production build process. This will include all `js`, `css`, `png`, `jpg`, and `gif` assets. During this process, all these files will have an md5 checksum appended at the end of their filenames. During this process, all HTML and `css` files will be rewritten to include these new names.

There are several options available when fingerprinting a file. This is all controlled in the `ember-cli-build.js` file. Let's suppose that you wanted to disable fingerprinting:

```
...
fingerprint: {
 enabled: false
}
...
```

Another useful option is to prepend a domain to all static files. This can be done using the `prepend` option. Once again, this needs to be added to the `ember-cli-build.js` file in the root of the `application` folder:

```
...
fingerprint: {
    prepend: 'http://www.example.com'
}
```

Now, all assets will include the `www.example.com` domain. For example, a normal JavaScript `src` file will look like this:

```
<script src="assets/script.js">
```

This will be transformed into the following:

```
<script src="http://www.example.com/script-12324adfasdf123234.js">
```

Another useful option is `exclude`. This accepts an array of strings. Any filename in the `exclude` array will not be fingerprinted:

```
fingerprint: {
  exclude: ['fonts/12424']
}
```

The `ignore` option also accepts an array of strings. Any filename that contains any item in the `ignore` array will not be processed or fingerprinted:

```
fingerprint: {
  ignore: ['fonts/12424']
}
```

The `extension` option defaults to `'js'`, `'css'`, `'png'`, `'jpg'`, `'gif'`, and `'map'`. This option can be used to add other file types to get fingerprinted:

```
fingerprint: {
  extension: ['r3','html']
}
```

The `replaceExtensions` option defaults to `'html'`, `'css'`, and `'js'`. If needed, new file types can be added to replace source code with new checksum file names:

```
fingerprint: {
  replaceExtensions: ['html','htm']
}
```

How it works...

The import process is done via the Broccoli asset pipeline library. This build tool performs all the fingerprinting, minifying, and importing of the assets. In addition, Broccoli handles all the preprocessors if the appropriate plugins are installed.

The asset manifest is located in the `ember-cli-build.js` file in the root of the project folder. You can only import assets that are in the `bower_components` or `vendor` directories.

Dependency management

Let's look at dependency management and how we can use it in our Ember projects.

How to do it...

Bower is used for dependency management for Ember CLI. Bower is a frontend tool that is used to help fetch and install packages that you might need.

1. The `bower.json` file is located in the `root` folder of your project. It contains all the dependencies. Let's say that we want to install the **Bootstrap library**:

    ```
    $ bower install bootstrap --save
    ```

    This command will install `bootstrap` in the `bower_components` folder and save the package information in the `bower.json` file.

Ember add-ons

Another popular way of adding third-party libraries to Ember is using add-ons or addons as you sometimes see it. An add-on is Ember's way of sharing libraries between applications. There are well over a thousand of them available.

You can install add-ons using Ember CLI. For example, to install Bootstrap, you'd type this on the command line in the project directory:

```
$ ember install ember-bootstrap
```

You can easily find a list of add-ons at these websites:

http://www.emberobserver.com

http://www.emberaddons.com

This will be discussed in more detail in the *Working and creating add-ons* recipe in *Chapter 11, Real-Time Web Applications*.

2. If, for some reason, you need to reinstall your dependencies, you can run the install command by itself:

```
$ bower install
```

This will install all dependencies that are listed in the bower.json file.

The app.import code

Ember CLI allows you to load **Asynchronous Module Definition** (**AMD**) and non-AMD assets. It's a way of defining code modules and their dependencies.

1. To load a non-AMD asset, you'll need to import it using the ember-cli-build.js file:

```
...
app.import('bower_components/moment/moment.js');
```

2. This is useful as you can use Bower to install components, and then use the app. import AMD so that it's available in the program. You'll need to consult the package specification to see how to use it.

Tip on JSHint

JSHint is a community-driven tool that detects errors and potential problems with JavaScript code. It's built-in in Ember CLI. When using non-AMD assets, you may get errors with JSHint if you have global variables. To fix this, add /* global MY_GLOBAL */ at the top of your module page. In the moment example, it would look like /* global moment */.

3. AMD assets are imported in a similar way. You add the path in the first argument and a list of exports and modules in the second:

```
app.import('bower_components/ic-ajax/dist/named-amd/main.js', {
  exports: {
    'ic-ajax': [
      'default',
      'defineFixture',
      'lookupFixture',
      'raw',
      'request',
    ]
  }
});
```

4. To use this asset in your application, you can import it as follows:

```
import { raw as icAjaxRaw } from 'ic-ajax';;
```

How it works...

Dependency management is done via Bower. After the dependency is installed, the Broccoli library is called on to add the assets to the pipeline. Both these tools are written in node and are built-in in Ember CLI.

Upgrading your project

Ember CLI is constantly being upgraded and every six weeks Ember.js has another release. It is important to keep your build tools and versions up to date. In this recipe we'll look at the best way of doing this.

How to do it...

To upgrade your Ember CLI version, you must perform the following steps:

1. Begin by uninstalling the old `ember-cli`:

```
$ npm uninstall -g ember-cli
```

2. Clear the npm cache:

```
$ npm cache clean
```

3. Clear the Bower cache:

```
$ bower cache clean
```

4. Install the latest version of `ember-cli`:

   ```
   $ npm install -g ember-cli
   ```

5. If you need, you can specify the version to use represented by X.X.X:

   ```
   $ npm install -g ember-cli@X.X.X
   ```

Updating an existing project

In some situations, you might want to take an existing project and update it to the latest version of Ember CLI. In this case, you'll need to perform the following steps:

1. Begin by changing directories that you want to upgrade in the root of the project folder. Delete these temporary development directories:

   ```
   $ rm -rf node_modules bower_components dist tmp
   ```

2. Update the `package.json` file with the version of Ember that we're upgrading to using this command:

   ```
   $ npm install ember-cli@X.X.X --save-dev
   ```

   X.X.X represents the version of `ember-cli`. The `--save-dev` argument will save the information in the `package.json` file.

3. Install all the npm and Bower packages again:

   ```
   $ npm install
   $ bower install
   ```

4. The last step is to run the `init` command:

   ```
   $ ember init
   ```

   The `init` command will add the default project blueprint to your directory.

init

The `init` command will create a new application blueprint in your project directory. Follow the prompts and review all the changes. You may be asked to replace existing files. Press *d* to do a diff of the files and review the changes made. Create a backup of your project before you begin the upgrade process.

Keep in mind that after upgrading your project, you might have many new deprecation warnings to deal with. You will see these warnings when you run `ember server`. Each one will need to be addressed.

To address these deprecations, view the warnings that the applications provide. For instance, you may get a warning about `Ember.View`. The warning will describe that `Ember.Component` should be used instead. You'll then need to swap out the effected code with Ember components instead of Ember views.

How it works...

When you upgrade the tool, you are simply uninstalling the node package and reinstalling the latest one. It's a good idea to clear the Bower and Node cache as well so that Node and Bower won't have any conflicting packages.

When we update an existing project we first have to make sure that all the existing modules and packages are deleted. This is important because when we install the latest version of Ember CLI, some packages might change. After `ember-cli` is saved back in the package file, then you can install `npm` and Bower again.

Running `ember init` generates the application structure in the directory that you're in. This is important because some files may have changed since the last upgrade. You can always press *d* to diff the changes.

Deployment

After creating your application you'll need to be able to deploy it. Let's take a look at a few ways to deploy your application.

How to do it...

1. The first fundamental step before deployment is building your project. To build your application, run the `build` command:

   ```
   $ ember build
   ```

2. This command builds the contents of the project in the `/dist` folder. To build your project for production, you'll need to use the `-prod` argument:

   ```
   $ ember build -prod
   ```

3. If you need, you can designate the default output folder:

   ```
   $ ember build -prod -o<directory>
   ```

Building your application for production will automatically minify your files as well as fingerprint them. This does not occur when your environment is set up for development, which is set by default.

The `/dist` folder has everything that your web server needs. At this point, to deploy your application, all you need to do is copy the contents of the `/dist` folder to your web server.

Ember CLI Deploy

Another great way to deploy your Ember application is to use the Ember add-on called **Ember CLI Deploy**. This add-on helps you deploy your Ember application to a number of different services. It has a very active community behind it so you can expect frequent updates. As your Ember applications grows you may want to take a look at this. You can find more information about Ember CLI deploy here: `https://github.com/ember-cli/ember-cli-deploy`.

Deploying to Firebase

Firebase is a backend service that can handle data storage, user authentication, static hosting, and more. For this example we'll be using Firebase as a way to host our Ember application.

1. Sign up for an account with Firebase. This can be done at `http://www.firebase.com`.

2. Next, install the `firebase-tools`:

   ```
   $ npm install -g firebase-tools
   ```

3. After you have a project created and you're ready to deploy, run the `firebase init` command in the root of the folder:

   ```
   $ firebase init
   ```

   After running this command, you'll be asked a few questions. It will first ask you to sign in to your Firebase account. Enter your credentials to continue. Then, it will ask for the name of your Firebase application. Lastly, it will ask for the name of your app's public directory. In most cases, this should be `/dist`.

4. Edit the `firebase.json` file and add some rewrite rules:

   ```
   {
     "firebase": "my-new-app",
     "public": "dist",
     "rewrites": [{
       "source": "**",
       "destination": "/index.html"
     }],
   }
   ```

   This is needed to help with navigation in the application. Change `my-new-app` to the name of your app as well.

5. All that's left is to deploy to Firebase:

   ```
   $ firebase deploy
   ```

How it works...

The Ember CLI build process is compiled using the Broccoli asset pipeline and the build tool itself. It takes all the files and minifies, fingerprints, and organizes them in the /dist folder so that it is ready to be deployed.

Many services exist that can host static files. You can use Firebase or just host it in your own Nginx or Apache server after building it for production.

2

The Ember.Object Model

In this chapter, we will cover the following recipes:

- ▶ Working with classes and instances
- ▶ Working with computed properties
- ▶ Working with Ember observers in Ember.js
- ▶ Working with bindings
- ▶ Using mixins
- ▶ Using enumerables with arrays

Introduction

Ember.Object is the base class for almost every other Ember object. Routes, models, views, and components all inherit from Ember.Object. It's used everywhere so it's important to understand how it works and how it can be used in our application.

Standard JavaScript objects aren't used often in Ember. Ember's object model builds on JavaScript objects and adds important features such as observers, mixins, computed properties, and initializers. Many of these features are aligned to be in the new **ECMAScript** standard.

Working with classes and instances

Creating and extending classes is a major feature of the Ember object model. In this recipe, we'll take a look at how creating and extending objects works.

How to do it...

1. Let's begin by creating a very simple `Ember` class using `extend()`:

```
const Light = Ember.Object.extend({
  isOn: false
});
```

This defines a new `Light` class with a property called `isOn`. `Light` inherits properties and behavior from the Ember object, such as initializers, mixins, and computed properties.

Ember Twiddle tip

At any point of time, you might need to test out small snippets of the Ember code. An easy way to do this is to use a website called **Ember Twiddle**. From this website, you can create an Ember application and run it in the browser as if you were using the Ember CLI. You can even save and share it. It has similar tools such as JSFiddle but only for Ember. Check it out at `http://ember-twiddle.com`.

2. Once you have defined a class, you'll need to be able to create an instance of it. You can do this using the `create()` method. We'll go ahead and create an instance of `Light`:

```
constbulb = Light.create();
```

Accessing properties within the bulb instance

1. We can access the properties of the `bulb` object using the `set` and `get` accessor methods. Let's go ahead and get the `isOn` property of the `Light` class:

```
console.log(bulb.get('isOn'));
```

The preceding code will get the `isOn` property from the `bulb` instance.

2. To change the `isOn` property, we can use the `set` accessor method:

```
bulb.set('isOn', true)
```

The `isOn` property will now be set to `true` instead of `false`.

Initializing the Ember object

The `init` method is invoked whenever a new instance is created. This is a great place to put in any code that you may need for the new instance.

1. In our example, we'll add an alert message that displays the default setting for the `isOn` property:

```
const Light = Ember.Object.extend({
  init(){
    alert('The isON property is defaulted to ' +
      this.get('isOn'));
  },
  isOn: false
});
```

2. As soon as the `Light.create` line of code is executed, the instance will be created and **The isON property is defaulted to false** message will pop up on the screen.

Subclass

Be aware that you can create subclasses of your objects in Ember. You can override methods and access the parent class using the `_super()` keyword method. This is done by creating a new object that uses the Ember `extend` method on the parent class.

Another important thing is if you're subclassing a framework class such as `Ember.Component` and you override the `init` method, you'll need to make sure that you call `this._super()`. If not, the component might not work properly.

Reopening classes

At any time, you can reopen a class and define new properties or methods in it. For this, use the `reopen` method.

In our previous example, we had an `isON` property. Let's reopen the same class and add a `color` property:

1. To add the `color` property, we need to use the `reopen()` method:

```
Light.reopen({
  color: 'yellow'
});
```

2. If needed, you can add static methods or properties using `reopenClass`:

```
Light.reopenClass({
  wattage: 80
});
```

3. You can now access the static property `Light.wattage`.

How it works...

In the previous examples, we created an Ember object using `extend`. This tells Ember to create a new `Ember` class. The `extend` method uses inheritance in the Ember.js framework. The `Light` object inherits all the methods and bindings of the Ember object.

The `create` method also inherits from the Ember object class and returns a new instance of this class. The `bulb` object is a new instance of the Ember object that we created.

There's more...

To use the previous examples, we can create our own module and import it to our project.

1. To do this, create a new file in the `app` folder called `MyObject.js`:

```
// app/myObject.js
import Ember from 'ember';
export default function() {
    const Light = Ember.Object.extend({
      init(){
        alert('The isON property is defaulted to ' +
          this.get('isOn'));
      },
      isOn: false
    });

    Light.reopen({
      color: 'yellow'
    });

    Light.reopenClass({
      wattage: 80
    });

    const bulb = Light.create();
```

```
    console.log(bulb.get('color'));
    console.log(Light.wattage);
}
```

This is a module that we can now import to any file in our Ember application.

2. In the `app` folder, edit the `app.js` file. You'll need to add the following line at the top of the file:

```
// app/app.js
import myObject from './myObject';
```

3. At the bottom, before the export, add this line:

```
myObject();
```

This will execute the `myObject` function that we created in the `myObject.js` file. After running `ember server`, you'll see the `isOn` property defaulted to a `false` popup message.

Working with computed properties

In this recipe, we'll take a look at computed properties and how they can be used to display data, even if that data changes as the application is running.

How to do it...

Let's create a new Ember.Object and add a computed property to it:

1. Let's begin by creating a new `description` computed property. This property will reflect the status of the `isOn` and `color` properties:

```
const Light = Ember.Object.extend({
  isOn: false,
  color: 'yellow',

  description: Ember.computed('isOn','color',function() {
    return 'The ' + this.get('color') + ' light is set to '
      + this.get('isOn');
  })

});
```

2. We can now create a new `Light` object and get the computed property `description`:

```
const bulb = Light.create();
bulb.get('description'); //The yellow light is set to false
```

The preceding example creates a computed property that depends on the `isOn` and `color` properties. When the `description` function is called, it returns a string describing the state of the light.

Computed properties will observe changes and dynamically update whenever they occur.

3. To see this in action, we can change the preceding example and set the `isOn` property to `false`. Use the following code to accomplish this:

```
bulb.set('isOn', true);
bulb.get('description') //The yellow light is set to true
```

The description has been automatically updated and will now display `The yellow light is set to true`.

Chaining the Light object

Ember provides you with a nice feature that allows computed properties to be present in other computed properties. In the previous example, we created a `description` property that outputted some basic information about the `Light` object.

1. Let's add another property that gives a full description:

```
const Light = Ember.Object.extend({
  isOn: false,
  color: 'yellow',
  age: null,

  description: Ember.computed('isOn','color',function() {
    return 'The ' + this.get('color') + ' light is set to '
      + this.get('isOn');
  }),

  fullDescription:
    Ember.computed('description','age',function() {
    return this.get('description') + ' and the age is ' +
      this.get('age')
  }),

});
```

2. The `fullDescription` function returns a string that concatenates the output from the description with a new string that displays `age`:

```
const bulb = Light.create({age:22});
bulb.get('fullDescription');
    //The yellow light is set to false and the age is 22
```

In this example, during the instantiation of the `Light` object, we set the `age` to `22`. We could have overwritten any property if necessary.

Alias

The `Ember.computed.alias` method allows us to create a property that is an alias for another property or object.

1. Any call to `get` or `set` will behave as if the changes were made to the original property:

```
const Light = Ember.Object.extend({
  isOn: false,
  color: 'yellow',
  age: null,
  description: Ember.computed('isOn','color',function() {
    return 'The ' + this.get('color') + ' light is set to '
      + this.get('isOn');
  }),
  fullDescription:
    Ember.computed('description','age',function() {
    return this.get('description') + ' and the age is ' +
      this.get('age')
  }),
  aliasDescription: Ember.computed.alias('fullDescription')
});

const bulb = Light.create({age: 22});
bulb.get('aliasDescription');
    //The yellow light is set to false and the age is 22.
```

2. The `aliasDescription` alias will display the same text as `fullDescription` as it's just an alias of this object. If we made any changes to any properties in the `Light` object later, the alias would also observe these changes and be computed properly. We'll discuss more about this in the *Working with bindings* recipe.

How it works...

Computed properties are built on top of the observer pattern. Whenever an observation shows a state change, it recomputes the output. If no changes occur, then the result is cached.

In other words, computed properties are functions that get updated whenever any of their dependent values change. You can use them in much the same way that you would use a static property. They are common and useful throughout Ember and its codebase.

Keep in mind that a computed property will only update if it is in a template or function that is being used. If the function or template is not being called, nothing will occur. This will help with performance.

Working with Ember observers in Ember.js

Observers are fundamental to the Ember object model. In the next recipe, we'll take our light example, add an observer, and see how it operates.

How to do it...

1. To begin, we'll add a new observer called `isOnChanged`. This will only trigger when the `isOn` property changes:

```
const Light = Ember.Object.extend({
  isOn: false,
  color: 'yellow',
  age: null,
  description: Ember.computed('isOn','color',function() {
    return 'The ' + this.get('color') + '
      light is set to ' + this.get('isOn')
  }),
  fullDescription: Ember.computed
    ('description','age',function() {
    return this.get('description') + ' and the age is ' +
      this.get('age')
  }),
  desc: Ember.computed.alias('description'),
  isOnChanged: Ember.observer('isOn',function() {
    console.log('isOn value changed')
  })
});

const bulb = Light.create({age: 22});

bulb.set('isOn',true); //console logs isOn value changed
```

`Ember.observer` `isOnChanged` monitors the `isOn` property. If any changes occur to this property, `isOnChanged` is invoked.

Computed properties versus observers

At first glance, it might seem that observers are the same as computed properties. In fact, they are very different. Computed properties can use `get` and `set` methods and can be used in templates. Observers, on the other hand, just monitor property changes and cannot be used in templates or be accessed like properties. They don't return any values as well. With this said, be careful not to overuse observers. In many instances, a computed property is a more appropriate solution.

2. Additionally, if needed, you can add multiple properties to the observer. Just use the following code:

```
Light.reopen({
isAnythingChanged: Ember.observer('isOn','color',function() {
    console.log('isOn or color value changed')
  })
});

const bulb = Light.create({age: 22});
bulb.set('isOn',true); // console logs isOn or color value changed
bulb.set('color','blue'); // console logs isOn or color
  value changed
```

The `isAnything` observer is invoked whenever the `isOn` or `color` properties change. The observer will fire twice as each property has changed.

Synchronous issues with the Light object and observers

It's very easy to get observers out of sync. If, for example, a property that it observes changes, it will be invoked as expected. After being invoked, it might manipulate a property that hasn't been updated yet. This can cause synchronization issues as everything happens at the same time.

1. The following example shows this behavior:

```
Light.reopen({
  checkIsOn: Ember.observer('isOn', function() {
    console.log(this.get('fullDescription'));
  })
});

const bulb = Light.create({age: 22});
bulb.set('isOn', true);
```

When isOn is changed it's not clear if fullDescription, a computed property, has been updated yet or not. As observers work synchronously, it's difficult to tell what has been fired and changed. This can lead to unexpected behavior.

2. To counter this, it's best to use the Ember.run.once method. This method is a part of the Ember run loop, which is Ember's way of managing how code gets executed. Reopen the Light object and you will see the following:

```
Light.reopen({
    checkIsOn: Ember.observer('isOn','color', function() {
      Ember.run.once(this,'checkChanged');
    }),
    checkChanged: Ember.observer('description',function() {
      console.log(this.get('description'));
    })
});
const bulb = Light.create({age: 22});
bulb.set('isOn', true);
bulb.set('color', 'blue');
```

The checkIsOn observer calls the checkChanged observer using Ember.run. once. This method gets run only once per run loop. Normally, checkChanged would get fired twice; however, as it's being called using Ember.run.once, it outputs only once.

How it works...

Ember observers are mixins from the Ember.Observable class. They work by monitoring property changes. When any change occurs, they are triggered. Keep in mind that these are not the same as computed properties and cannot be used in templates or with getters or setters.

Working with bindings

Most frameworks include some sort of binding implementation. Ember is no exception and has bindings that can be used with any object. The following recipes explain how to use them as well as one-way and two-way binding.

How to do it...

In this example, there is a teacher and student Ember object. Each has its own set of properties and they both have homeroom. We can share the homeroom by setting an alias for the teacher object.

1. Let's begin by creating a teacher and student `Ember.Object`:

```
const Teacher = Ember.Object.extend({
    homeroom: '',
    age: '',
    gradeTeaching: ''
});

const Student = Ember.Object.extend({
    homeroom: Ember.computed.alias('teacher.homeroom'),
    age: '',
    grade: '',
    teacher: null
});
```

The student `homeroom` is `Ember.computed.alias`, which will bind the `homeroom` property to `teacher.homeroom`.

2. Next, we'll instantiate the `teacher` and `student` objects:

```
const avery = Teacher.create({
    age: '27',
    homeroom: '1075',
    gradeTeaching: 'sophmore'
});

const joey = student.create({
    age: '16',
    grade: 'sophmore',
    teacher: avery
});
```

The `joey` object has the `homeroom` property set to `avery`, which is the `teacher` object that we just created.

3. We can now use `console.log` to output our findings:

```
console.log(joey.get('age')); //16
console.log(avery.get('homeroom')); //1075
avery.set('homeroom','2423');
console.log(joey.get('homeroom')); //2423
```

As you can see, whenever the `avery` object changes its `homeroom`, the student `joey` homeroom changes as well. This is because the homeroom for joey is an alias for the teacher, `avery`.

4. You do not always have to access properties that reference other objects. You can bind to anything:

```
const myName = Ember.Object.extend({
  name: 'Erik Hanchett',
  otherName: Ember.computed.alias('name')
});

const erik = myName.create();

console.log(erik.get('name')); //Erik Hanchett
console.log(erik.get('otherName')); //Erik Hanchett
```

The alias points to `name`; therefore, when printing to the console, it shows `Erik Hanchett` for both.

 Ember has a class called `Ember.Binding`. This is a public class that has very similar behavior and functionality as `Ember.computed.alias` and `Ember.computed.oneWay`. You should use `Ember.computed.alias` and not `Ember.Binding`. Computed aliases are the preferred method of binding in Ember. `Ember.Binding` is still around and will probably be deprecated at some point.

One-way binding

Ember defaults to something called two-way binding. What this means is that when properties are changed in the UI, this is updated back in the controller or component. On the other hand, one-way binding propagates changes in one direction only.

For instance, let's say that we have a `User` object with a `firstName`, `lastName`, and `nickName` property. We can use `Ember.computed.oneWay` to create a one-way binding for the `firstName` property.

Let's see what happens when we try to make a change to it. Create a new user object with these properties. Instantiate the object and try changing the properties:

```
const User = Ember.Object.extend({
  firstName: null,
  lastName: null,
  nickName: Ember.computed.oneWay('firstName')
});

const user = User.create({
  firstName: 'Erik',
  lastName: 'Hanchett'
});
```

```
console.log(user.get('nickName'));          // 'Erik'
user.set('nickName', 'Bravo'); // 'Bravo'
console.log(user.get('firstName'));         // 'Erik'
```

You can see that `nickName` does not change even though user has been updated. You can think of one-way binding like using `Ember.computed.alias`. However, it allows you to get values only and not set them. The upstream properties don't get changed when using `Ember.computed.oneWay`.

How it works...

Ember bindings are used in many parts of the Ember framework. They are derived from the `Ember.computed` namespace. In this namespace is the computed alias method. A computed alias specifies the path to another object by creating a two-way binding.

Binding objects don't update immediately. Ember waits until all the application code has finished running before synchronizing all the changes. This prevents unneeded overhead of syncing bindings when values are being updated.

One-way binding works by information being propagated only one way. Information does not get updated in the upstream properties.

Using mixins

Mixins are a great way of reusing and sharing code in Ember. The following recipes go over some basic operations on how to use them in your code.

How to do it...

In this recipe, we'll create a common mixin object.

1. Create an Ember mixin object that has a couple of properties and a function:

```
const common = Ember.Mixin.create({
    property1: 'This is a mixin property',
    edit: function() {
      console.log('Starting to edit');
      this.set('isEditing', true);
    },
    isEditing: false
});
```

This mixin can be added to any object. For the sake of simplicity, all this mixin does is display some text and set the `isEditing` property to `true` if the `edit` function is invoked.

2. Let's see what it looks like when we add this object to an object:

```
const obj = Ember.Object.extend(common, {
  objprop: 'This is an Ember object property'
});

const object = obj.create();
```

The `extend` method present in `Ember.Object` allows for one or more optional arguments of the `Ember.Mixin` type. In this example, we added the common mixin to the new `Ember.Object` object. We then instantiated this Ember object using `create`.

3. All that's left is to output the contents. Use `console.log` to display each property:

```
console.log(object.get('objprop'));  //This is an Ember object
  property
console.log(object.get('property1'));  //This is a mixin property
console.log(object.get('isEditing'));  //false
object.edit();  //Starting to edit
console.log(object.get('isEditing')); //true
```

This is what the output will look like. As you can see, we can access any of the mixin properties or methods as if the mixin was included in the Ember object itself. This is a convenient way of reusing code in your applications.

4. Let's create another mixin:

```
const secondMixin = Ember.Mixin.create({
  secondProperty: 'This is the second mixin property'
});
```

5. Now let's see how this looks if we add it to an Ember object:

```
const obj = Ember.Object.extend(common, secondMixin, {
  objprop: 'This is an Ember object Property'
});
```

6. Now, we can have access to both the common and `secondMixin` in our object. We can use `console.log` to output `secondProperty`:

```
console.log(object.get('secondProperty'));
  //This is the    second mixin propety
```

Mixins with the Ember CLI

Mixins work very well with the Ember CLI. To start, use the mixin generator to create one.

1. Make sure that you're in the application directory, and then type the following command:

```
$ ember generate mixin common
installing mixin
   create app/mixins/common.js
installing mixin-test
   create tests/unit/mixins/common-test.js
```

The `generator` command creates an `app/mixins` folder and the `common.js` file. The `common.js` file is where we will put the code for the mixin.

2. We'll use the mixin from the previous example and add it to this file:

```
// app/mixins/common.js
import Ember from 'ember';

export default Ember.Mixin.create({
    property1: 'This is a mixin property',
    edit: function() {
      console.log('Starting to edit');
      this.set('isEditing', true);
    },
    isEditing: false
});
```

This mixin is exactly the same as the previous example; however, now it's in a module that we can import anywhere, including components or controllers.

For now, we'll import it to our `app.js` file in the `app` folders directory.

3. First, we'll need to add the `import` statement to the top of the file:

```
import common from './mixins/common';
```

This allows us to use the common mixin anywhere in the `app.js` file.

4. We'll add the following code to the bottom of the `app/app.js` file:

```
// app/app.js

const obj = Ember.Object.extend(common, {
  objprop: 'This is an Ember object property'
});
```

```
const object = obj.create();

console.log(object.get('objprop'));
  //This is an Ember object property
console.log(object.get('property1'));
  //This is a mixin property
console.log(object.get('isEditing'));
  //false
object.edit();  //Starting to edit
console.log(object.get('isEditing'));  //true
```

As you can see, all the properties and methods in the common mixin are available to the object.

5. If we were to add the common mixin to a component, it might look like following code. Add this code to the `common-example.js` file:

```
// app/components/common-example.js
import Ember from 'ember';
import common from '../mixins/common';

export default Ember.Component.extend(common,{
    compprop: 'This is a component property',
    actions: {
      pressed: function(){
        this.edit();
      }
    }
});
```

As always, we must first import the mixin to our component. The path is always relative to the directory you're in, therefore, we must use `../mixins/common` to find it.

In the component, I added a simple action called `pressed` that triggers the mixin `edit` method. If the action gets triggered, we would see the `Starting to edit` `message` in the console. Look for more examples of components in *Chapter 6, Ember Components*.

How it works...

The `Ember.Mixin` class allows the creation of mixins whose properties and methods can be added to other classes. They can't be instantiated but they can be added or *mixed in*.

A mixin in computer science is a class that lends or copies it's behavior to a borrowing class using composition instead of inheritance. It encourages code reuse and avoids ambiguity that multiple inheritance can cause.

Using enumerables with arrays

The `Ember.Enumerable` methods are very important when dealing with arrays. In these recipes, we'll look at some common use cases.

Getting ready

To understand how to use enumerables, we must first take a look at the standard JavaScript array methods and their equivalents using observable enumerables:

Standard method	Observable equivalent
unshift	unshiftObject
shift	shiftObject
reverse	reverseObjects
push	pushObject
pop	popObject

We'll be using some of these methods in our examples, so keep in mind what the standard and observable equivalents are.

The `Ember.Enumerable` class has several methods that we can use in our Ember applications. Here is the list of the more common methods and what they do:

Enumerable method	Definition
forEach	This iterates through the enumerable, calling the passed function on each item
firstObject	This returns the first object in a collection
lastObject	This returns the last object in a collection
map()	This maps all the items in the enumeration to another value, similar to map in JavaScript 1.6
mapBy()	Similar to map, this returns the value of the named property on all items on the enumeration
filter	This returns an array with all of the items in the enumeration that the passed function returns true
find	This returns the first item in the array that the method returns true

Enumerable method	Definition
findby	This returns the first item with a property that matches the passed value
every	This returns true only if the passed function returns true for every item in the enumeration
any	This returns true only if the passed function returns true for any item in the enumeration

Many of these methods are similar to their JavaScript counterparts. If you know how to use the JavaScript method, you should be able to use the Ember equivalent as well.

How to do it...

`Ember.Enumerables` adds all the nice features of Ember objects to enumerables. We'll take a look at several examples on how to do this. The contents for all these recipes are in the `chapter2/example6` folder in the `app.js` file.

Using forEach with an array

A very common use case for an enumerable is iterating over an array with `forEach`.

1. Create an array of students:

```
const students = ['Erik', 'Jim', 'Shelly', 'Kate'];
```

2. Use the `forEach` enumerable to iterate over the array:

```
students.forEach(function(item, index) {
  console.log(`Student #${index+1}: ${item}`);
});
```

The console output will show each student's name in the array:

```
Student #1: Erik
Student #2: Jim
Student #3: Shelly
Student #4: Kate
```

Template literals

Ember is compatible with the latest in ECMAScript 2015. One neat new feature is called template literals or template strings. Template literals are string literals that can stretch across multiple lines and include interpolated expressions. You can do string interpolation by surrounding variables in your strings, like this $ { }. Each variable will be displayed in the string as shown in the preceding `forEach` example.

Using map with an array

The `map` method takes an array, maps each item, and returns a new modified array. Let's say that we want to make the student names all in uppercase. We can do this using `map`.

1. Create a list of `students`:

   ```
   const students = ['Erik', 'Jim', 'Shelly', 'Kate'];
   ```

   The first letter is capitalized; however, we want all the letters in uppercase.

2. Use `map` to convert every item to uppercase:

   ```
   const upperCaseStudent= students.map(function(item) {
     return item.toUpperCase();
   });
   ```

   Every item in the array has been converted to uppercase. The new `upperCaseStudent` array has all the new values.

3. Use the `forEach` enumerable to iterate through every item in the array and display its contents:

   ```
   upperCaseStudent.forEach(function(item, index) {
     console.log(`student #${index+1}: ${item}`);
   });
   ```

   The output displays each name in the new `upperCaseStudent` array:

   ```
   student #1: ERIK
   student #2: JIM
   student #3: SHELLY
   student #4: KATE
   ```

Using mapBy with an array

The `mapBy` enumerable can be used if your array is comprised of objects. From each object, we can extract its named properties and return a new array.

1. Let's create a teacher and student object:

```
const student = Ember.Object.extend({
  name: 'Erik Hanchett'
});

const teacher = Ember.Object.extend({
  name: 'John P. Smith'

});
```

   Each object has one property called `name`:

2. Next we'll instantiate each object.

```
const t= teacher.create();
const s = student.create();
const people = [s, t];
```

   Each object is put into a `people` array:

3. We can use `mapBy` to create a new array.

```
console.log(people.mapBy('name'));
  //['Erik Hanchett', 'John P.    Smith']
```

   This new array returned has the values from the `name` property from both objects.

Finding the first and last objects in an array

If necessary, we have an easy way to grab the first and last objects in an array.

1. We'll begin by creating a student array:

```
const students = ['Erik', 'Jim', 'Shelly', 'Kate', 'Jenny',
  'Susan'];
```

   This array has six different students.

2. Let's grab the last object in the array:

```
console.log(students.get('lastObject')); //Susan
```

   This will display `Susan`, the last object in the array.

3. Now let's retrieve the first object in the array:

```
console.log(students.get('firstObject')); //Erik
```

This will display `Erik`, the first item in the array.

4. We can push objects on the array as well:

```
students.pushObject('Jeff');
```

5. The student `Jeff` has now been added to the list:

```
console.log(students.get('lastObject')); //Jeff
```

Fun with filters

A very common practice is to take an array and return a filtered list of items.

1. To begin, create an array of numbers:

```
const array = [1,2,5,10,25,23];
```

2. Take the `array` and `filter` it, returning only those numbers over `10`:

```
const newArray =array.filter(function(item, index, self) {
   return item > 10;
})
```

3. Use `console.log` to display the new array:

```
console.log(newArray); //[25,23]
```

This new array has numbers only greater then 10 in it.

Using filterBy with a collection of objects

With `filterBy`, you can take a collection of objects and filter it by some property.

1. Create a new `student` object that has a `name` and `grade`:

```
const student = Ember.Object.extend({
   grade: null,
   name: null
});
```

2. Add the students to a new array:

```
const listOfStudents = [
   student.create({grade: 'senior', name: 'Jen Smith'}),
   student.create({grade: 'sophmore', name: 'Ben Shine'}),
   student.create({grade: 'senior', name: 'Ann Cyrus'})
];
```

3. Use `filterBy` to show the students who are seniors:

```
const newStudent =
   listOfStudents.filterBy('grade','senior');
```

This returns an array of students who are seniors.

4. We can double-check the output using `forEach`:

```
newStudent.forEach(function(item,index){
   console.log(item.get('name'));
});
Jen Smith
Ann Cyrus
```

Using find to get the first match

The `find` enumerable works very similarly to `filter` except that it stops after finding the first match.

1. Create an array of numbers:

```
const array = [1,2,5,10,25,23];
```

2. Use `array.find` to retrieve the first number in the list that is over `10`:

```
const newArray =array.find(function(item, index){
   return item > 10;
});
```

3. We'll then check the output of the new array:

```
console.log(newArray); //25
```

The answer is `25` as it's the first number in the list that is over `10`.

Using findBy with collections

The `findBy` enumerable works very similarly to `filterBy` except that it stops after finding the first match.

1. Create a new `student` object:

```
const student = Ember.Object.extend({
   grade: null,
   name: null
});
```

2. Next, create an array of students:

```
const listOfStudents = [
  student.create({grade: 'senior', name: 'Jen Smith'}),
  student.create({grade: 'sophmore', name: 'Ben Shine'}),
  student.create({grade: 'senior', name: 'Ann Cyrus'})
];
```

3. Use `findBy` to match only the properties that have `grade` of `senior`:

```
const newStudent = listOfStudents.findBy('grade','senior');
```

4. This will return the first student who is a senior:

```
console.log(newStudent.get('name')); //Jen Smith
```

`Jen Smith` is the first student who matches this criteria so it is returned to the `newStudent` array.

Learning with the every enumerable

The `every` enumerable will return `true` only if every item matches a certain condition.

1. Begin by creating an array of numbers:

```
const array = [11,25,23,30];
```

2. Use the `every` enumerable to check whether every item in the array is greater than `10`:

```
console.log(array.every(function(item, index, self) {
  return item > 10;
})); //returns true
```

This returns `true` because every item in the array is over `10`

Using any to find at least one match

The `any` enumerable will return `true` if at least one item matches a certain condition.

1. Once again, create a list of numbers:

```
const array = [1,2,5,10,25,23];
```

2. Use the `any` enumerable to check whether any of these numbers in this array are over `10`:

```
console.log(array.any(function(item, index, self) {
  return item > 10;
})); //returns true
```

This will return `true` because at least one number is above `10`.

How it works...

The `Ember.Enumerable` mixin is Ember's implementation of the array API defined up to JavaScript 1.8. It's applied automatically on page load so any method is available. In order for Ember to be able to observe changes in an enumerable, you must use `Ember.Enumerable`.

The enumerable API follows ECMAScript specifications as much as possible so it minimizes incompatibilities with the other libraries. It uses native browser implementations in arrays where available.

3

Ember Templates

In this chapter, we will cover the following recipes:

- ▸ Defining an application template
- ▸ Working with conditionals in templates
- ▸ Displaying a list of items
- ▸ Binding with element attributes and classes
- ▸ Working with HTML links inside templates
- ▸ Handling HTML actions
- ▸ Using template input helpers
- ▸ Using development helpers

Introduction

Ember applications use a templating engine to display HTML and dynamic content to the user. In Ember, this is done via the Handlebars templating library. This library takes Handlebars expressions and renders them to the screen using data binding.

HTMLbars is a variant of Handlebars that Ember uses as well. It has better performance and handles building the DOM in a more efficient manner. Keep in mind that for this chapter, we'll be using HTMLbars and Handlebars interchangeably as they essentially do the same thing.

In this chapter, we'll be going over how to use templates in our applications.

Defining an application template

To work with templates, we need to understand the basics on how properties bind with controllers and components. Here are a few recipes that go over how to accomplish this.

Getting ready

Before we get started, we'll need to generate a template.

1. We'll first create a new application using Ember CLI:

   ```
   $ ember new HelloWorldApp
   $ cd HelloWorldApp
   ```

   This command will generate a new application that we can use for this recipe.

2. Next, create a new route that will add a new template:

   ```
   $ ember g route helloworld
   ```

   This command will generate the template and routes file as well as unit tests. The template file is called `helloworld.hbs` and will be generated in the `app/templates` folder. The route file is called `helloworld.js` and is located in the `app/routes` folder. The `route.js` file will also get modified with the new `helloworld` route. We'll discuss more about routes in *Chapter 4, Ember Router*.

3. After this, we'll need to generate a `controller`:

   ```
   $ ember g controller helloworld
   ```

   This will generate a new file called `helloworld.js` in the `app/controller` folder and a unit test in `tests/unit/controllers`. We are now ready to continue.

How to do it...

Let's take a look at adding properties to our new template file.

1. Begin by editing the `helloworld.hbs` file. For this simple example, we'll create a string with the first and last name properties as follows:

   ```
   // app/templates/helloworld.hbs
   Hello World! My name is {{firstName}} {{lastName}}.
   {{outlet}}
   ```

   Handlebar expressions are surrounded by double curly braces {{ }} and backed by a context. A context is an object from which Handlebar expressions read their properties. In this example, the context is the controller. The {{outlet}} will render the template of any nested routes, which will be discussed in more detail later.

2. The controller will need to have the `firstName` and `lastName` properties so that they can be displayed in the template:

```
// app/controllers/helloworld.js
import Ember from 'ember';

export default Ember.Controller.extend({
    firstName: 'Erik',
    lastName: 'Hanchett'
});
```

The controller has the same name as the template. The template, by convention, will retrieve the properties from the controller of the same name. Each of them is bound to each other. If any changes occur to the data, the other values will change.

Using templates with components

Similar to controllers, we can create a component that can act as a context for the template. In the component, we can set up properties that can be accessed by the template later.

1. To create a new component, use the `generate component` command:

   $ ember g component hello-world

   All components must have a dash in their names. This command will create the `hello-world.js` file in the `app/components/hello-world.js` folder, a template file in the `app/components/hello-world.hbs` file, and an integration test file at `tests/integration/components/hello-world-test.js`.

2. Edit the `hello-world.hbs` file and add the hello world string:

   ```
   // app/templates/components/hello-world.hbs
   Hello World! My name is {{firstName}} {{lastName}}.
   {{yield}}
   ```

   The `firstName` and `lastName` parameters are retrieved from the component. The `yield` expression is used when the component is in the block form. We'll talk more about this in *Chapter 6, Ember Components*.

3. Add two properties to the component file, `hello-world.js`, the first one being `firstName` and the last one being `lastName`:

   ```
   // components/hello-world.js
   import Ember from 'ember';

   export default Ember.Component.extend({
       firstName: 'John',
       lastName: 'Smith'
   });
   ```

4. For the last part, all we need to do is add the component that we just created to one of our `application.hbs` files:

```
// app/templates/application.hbs
<h2 id="title">Welcome to Ember</h2>

{{hello-world}}
{{outlet}}
```

The `{{hello-world}}` Handlebar expression adds the component to the `application.hbs` file. The `hello-world` template will then be rendered here. The `{{outlet}}` template will render the nested routes under the `application` route.

5. Start the Ember server and navigate to `http://localhost:4200`.

6. After the Ember server is started, open a web browser at localhost port 4200. The message on the screen will show **Hello World! My name is John Smith**.

7. Navigate to `http://localhost:4200/helloworld` and you'll be greeted with two messages. The message on the screen will show **Hello World! My name is John Smith. Hello World! My name is Erik Hanchett**.

8. When the `helloworld` route is loaded, the application template is displayed. The `{{outlet}}` template then gets rendered with the contents of the `helloworld` template file. This is why both messages are displayed. Remember that all routes are nested under the `application` route.

How it works...

Ember.js uses the Handlebars templating library. This library provides you with a way to do data binding between the component or controller, also known as a context, and the template. This data binding occurs in both directions. In other words, changes to the data in the component or controller will be reflected in the template. Changes in the template to the data will be reflected in the controller or component.

In the previous simple example, the `firstName` and `lastName` properties in the component were accessed in the template with double curly braces `{{}}`. This is known as a Handlebars expression. The template is just regular HTML with embedded Handlebar expressions. Ember compiles these templates later on during the build process.

Working with conditionals in templates

Using conditionals is fundamental to using Ember's templating engine. In the following recipes, we'll take a look at conditionals and how they work with templates.

How to do it...

Let's take a look at a simple example that displays text if some property is true.

1. Create a new project and generate a new controller called `conditional`. Run this command in the root of the `application` folder to create `controller` and `template`:

    ```
    $ ember g controller conditional
    $ ember g template conditional
    ```

    This will create the conditional controller.

2. Update the `router.js` file with the new `conditional` route:

    ```
    // app/router.js
    ...
    Router.map(function() {
      this.route('conditional');
    });
    ```

    This will add a new `conditional` route. To access this route using the Ember server, open a web browser and navigate to `http://localhost:4200/conditional`.

3. Update the `conditional` controller with the `isHomeworkDone` property:

    ```
    // app/controllers/conditional.js
    import Ember from 'ember';

    export default Ember.Controller.extend({
        isHomeworkDone: true});
    ```

    This will create a new `isHomeworkDone` property and default it to `true`.

4. Update the conditional template so that it will display one message if `isHomeworkDone` is `true` and another message if it isn't:

    ```
    // app/templates/conditional.hbs
    Hello!
    {{#if isHomeworkDone}}
     Thanks for finishing the homework!
    {{else}}
     Please finish the homework
    {{/if}}
    ```

The {{if}} statement is a helper and must be surrounded by curly braces {{}} like any other Handlebar expression. It begins with a # sign, which indicates that it's a form of a block invocation. The {{/if}} statement closes the statement.

The preceding example shows two statements, {{if}} and {{else}}, both in the block form. Only the statement that is true will be displayed.

5. As we know from the controller earlier, if isHomeworkDone is true, the statement Thanks for finishing the homework! will be displayed after the template is rendered. On the other hand, if isHomeworkDone was false, the statement Please finish the homework will be displayed.

6. To test this example, navigate to the http://localhost:4200/conditional route. The {{outlet}} in application.hbs will render the conditional template inside of it.

Using inline invocation with templates

Inline invocation can be used to display data with if statements, all within one line of code.

1. We'll take the previous example and recreate it using inline invocation. Edit the condtional.hbs file in the app/templates folder with the new if statement using inline invocation:

```
// app/templates/conditional.hbs
Hello

{{if isHomeworkDone 'Thanks for finishing the homework!'
  'Please finish the homework'}}
```

2. When using inline invocation, you don't need to use the pound sign # or end the if block with {{/if}}. Everything can be written in one expression.

3. The first argument of the helper after isHomeworkDone, Thanks for finishing the homework!, will be shown only if isHomeworkDone is true. The second argument, Please finish the homework, will be displayed if isHomeworkDone is false.

Working on nested invocation with templates

Nested invocations are inline, which means that they return a single value. They can also accept multiple nested `if` statements in the inline helper.

1. In the `conditional` controller, add a couple of properties called `isHomeworkDone` and `isChoresDone`:

    ```
    // app/controllers/conditional.js
    import Ember from 'ember';

    export default Ember.Controller.extend({
        isHomeworkDone: true,
        isChoresDone: true});
    ```

    Both of these are defaulted to `true`.

2. Let's use nested invocation to display a message only if both `isHomeworkDone` and `isChoresDone` are `true`. Edit the `condtional.hbs` file with the new nested `if` statement:

    ```
    // app/templates/conditional.hbs
    Hello

    {{if isHomeworkDone (if isChoresDone 'Thanks for finishing the
        homework!' )}}
    ```

    The `Thanks for finishing the homework` string will display only if both `isChoresDone` and `isHomeworkDone` are `true`. Otherwise, nothing is displayed. As the controller has both values set to `true`, the message will display **Thanks for finishing the homework!** after the template is rendered.

The opposite of if is unless

Another useful helper is `unless`. It works exactly the opposite of the `if` helper. It can work with all three invocation styles—inline, block, and nested.

We'll create the `unless` block that will display a string if it's not true in our `conditional.hbs` file:

```
// app/templates/conditional.hbs
Hello

{{#unless isHomeworkDone}}
  Please finish the homework
{{else}}
  Thanks for finishing the homework!
{{/unless}}
```

In this block, the `unless` helper will display `Please finish the homework` only if `isHomeworkDone` is `false`. On the other hand, the message `Thanks for finishing the homework!` will be displayed if `isHomeworkDone` is `true`. This is essentially the opposite of the `if` helper.

In this example, assuming that `isHomeworkDone` is `true`, the `Thanks for finishing the homework!` string will be displayed in the template after it's rendered.

How it works...

The `if` and `unless` conditionals are built-in helpers that are made available to us from the Handlebars templating engine. They are surrounded by curly braces `{{}}`, which tell Handlebars to interpret them. The `{{if}}` statement checks whether the property is `true`. JavaScript values such as `undefined`, `null`, `''`, `[]`, and numeric `0` will return as `false`.

There are three different ways in which these conditional helpers can be invoked—block, nested, or inline. All three will work with `if` and `unless` helpers.

Displaying a list of items

Often, you'll have a list of items that you'll need to iterate over. We can iterate through these items with the `each` helper. This recipe will go over how to do this.

How to do it...

Let's say that we have a list of students and want to display them in our template. We'll use the `each` helper to accomplish this.

1. In a new project, generate `student controller` and `template`:

    ```
    $ ember g template student
    $ ember g controller student
    ```

    This will create the necessary files needed for our example.

2. Update the `router.js` file with the new `student` route:

    ```
    // app/router.js
    ...
    Router.map(function() {
      this.route('student');
    });
    ```

    This will add a new `conditional` route. To access this route using the Ember server, open a web browser and navigate to `http://localhost:4200/student`.

3. Update our student controller with an array of `students` as a property:

```
// app/controllers/students.js
import Ember from 'ember';

export default Ember.Controller.extend({
  students: [ {name: 'Erik'}, {name: 'Jim'}, {name:
    'Jane'}]
});
```

This array has three student objects.

4. In our `student.hbs` template, we'll iterate through the `students` array using the `each` helper:

```
// app/templates/student.hbs

{{#each students as |student|}}
  {{student.name}}<br>
{{/each}}
```

The first argument to the `each` helper is the array to be iterated over. In this case, this is the `students` array that was declared in the `student` controller. The `|student|` block `param` is what we'll use to iterate over the array.

The `each` helper must be in the block form. In this example, each value of the student will be displayed with an HTML break afterward.

5. The output will look like this after being rendered:

```
Erik<br>
Jim<br>
Jane<br>
```

If, by chance, the array was empty, you can use `{{else}}`.

6. Add a new array to the template. This array can be empty or may not even exist:

```
// app/templates/student.hbs

{{#each emptyArray as |item|}}
  {{item}}
{{else}}
  Empty Array
{{/each}}
```

The `else` block will be rendered only if the array is empty or doesn't exist.

Finding the index of the array

If needed, you can also access `index` of the array in the second block `param`.

1. Create a new array and add the `index` block `param`:

    ```
    // app/templates/student.hbs

    {{#each students as |student index|}}
    Student {{student.name}} is at index {{index}}<br>
    {{/each}}
    ```

    After each iteration, `name` and `index` is displayed with an HTML break element. The index can be accessed using the double curly braces `{{index}}`.

2. Assuming that we are using the same student array from earlier in this chapter, the rendered output will look as follows:

    ```
    Student Erik is at index 0<br>
    Student Jim is at index 1<br>
    Student Jane is at index 2<br>
    ```

    Keep in mind that `index` starts at `0` and not `1`.

How it works...

The `each` helper uses block params to iterate through arrays. The `each` helper takes an array argument and the block `param` is used to iterate each individual item on the list. If the array doesn't exist or is empty, you can use `else` to display a message instead.

In the recipes in this chapter, the `students` array was declared in `controller`. It had several student objects that could be accessed by the template. The template used this array and iterated over it with the `each` helper.

Binding with element attributes and classes

A very useful feature of HTMLBars is binding elements to attributes in your HTML.

How to do it...

A very simple example would be binding an element to an `img src` tag.

1. In a new project, generate `index template` and `index controller`:

    ```
    $ ember g template index
    $ ember g controller index
    ```

    This will generate the files needed for this example.

2. Create a new `index controller` file with `url`, `sideClass`, and `secondClass` as its properties:

```
// app/controllers/index.js
import Ember from 'ember';
export default Ember.Controller.extend({
  url: 'http://placehold.it/350x200',
  sideClass: 'cc',
  secondClass: 'dd'

});
```

We get the `index` route and controller without having to create a specific route for them. It works like the application route, which all other routes inherit from.

3. Create a new template and add an `img` tag. The `url` element will be displayed:

```
// app/templates/index.hbs


<img src="{{url}}"/>
```

This will be rendered as if the `url` property is in the `src` attribute for the `img` tag.

4. The template will be rendered with the `url` property as follows:

```
<img src="http://placehold.it/350x200"/>
```

We can essentially add this to any tag we like.

5. Let's create a `div` tag in our template with a couple of properties added for the class:

```
// app/templates/index.hbs

<div id="side" class="{{sideClass}}
  {{secondClass}}">Info</div>
```

Both `sideClass` and `secondClass` will be added to the class attribute. As these properties are bound, they act like any other property in Ember. They can be dynamically changed and the template will render accordingly.

Content security policy

When running examples in this book, you might occasionally see messages in the console warning you about content security violations. They'll usually appear in big red text in your console. The Ember team put this in place to help remind developers about potential security issues that your application might have. For the purpose of this book, these warnings can be ignored. On the other hand, you can fix these warnings by editing the `config/ environment.js` file and the `contentSecurityPolicy` section. You can find examples on how content security works at `http://content-security-policy.com/`.

How it works...

Binding elements in attributes is done by the HTMLBars templating library, which is based on the Handlebars library. It looks at every attribute with a property and renders it on the screen. These attributes are bound to properties that can be accessed in the controller or component.

We can bind any property to any attribute. The only exception being view helpers. We'll discuss this more in a later part of the chapter.

Working with HTML links inside templates

One of the most useful helpers that Ember.js provides is the link-to helper. We'll discuss how to use this helpful feature in this recipe.

How to do it...

The link-to helper is used to navigate an Ember application. The first argument is always the name of the route. The second is the dynamic segment. We'll discuss dynamic segments a little later.

One of the simplest ways to use the link-to helper is to use it inline.

1. Create a new student application and route. Run this command in the root of the project directory:

    ```
    $ ember g route students
    ```

    Ember CLI will generate a new route called students. This will update the router.js file as well as add the template and route files.

2. Open the students.hbs file in the app/templates folder and add this string to it:

    ```
    // app/templates/students.hbs
    Hi from the students route
    {{outlet}}
    ```

    This message will be displayed after navigating to the students route.

3. Open the application.hbs file. Let's add a link-to helper:

    ```
    // app/templates/application.hbs
    {{#link-to 'students'}}Students{{/link-to}}<br>
    {{outlet}}
    ```

    The link-to helper's first argument is students. This is the students route that we created earlier. This will render an HTML hyperlink with the name of Students linked to the students route. The {{outlet}} tells the Handlebars templating library where to render the output of the route.

4. The output of `link-to` will show an HTML link. When this is clicked, the link will display the `students` route message that we created earlier in the `students.hbs` file. This is rendered by `{{outlet}}`:

```
Students
Hi from the students route
```

`Students` is a hyperlink to the route, `/students`.

Ember.js is smart enough to remember the history of a link after it's clicked. Therefore, if by chance a user clicks back on the web browser, it will return to the previous route.

5. You can override this behavior, if needed, by adding the `replace=true` option to the `link-to` helper:

```
// app/templates/application.hbs
{{#link-to 'students' replace=true}}
  Students{{/link-to}}<br>
{{outlet}}
```

Adding data attributes to view helpers

Unfortunately, data view helpers such as `link-to` and `input` don't allow custom data attributes. In other words, if you're using `link-to`, you can't add `data-toggle='dropdown'` to the end of the `link-to` helper. Normal attributes such as class will work, however.

One way to add custom attributes is to reopen `Ember.LinkComponent` for `link-to` or `Ember.TextField` for the `input` helper. Reopening a class was discussed in *Chapter 2, The Ember.Object Model*, so check there first. After reopening the class, you can add an `attributeBindings` property array. Each element in the array is a data attribute that you want available to your `link-to` or `input` helper. For example, to add `data-toggle` as an attribute to your `link-to` helper, it would look like `attributeBindings: ['data-toggle']`. We'll discuss more about `input` helpers in the next section.

Alternatively, you can create a component that extends from `LinkComponent` instead of the normal simple component. You can then add attributes to it. Make sure to name it something other than `link-to`.

Using link-to helpers with dynamic segments

Link-to helpers can be used to link dynamic segments. The dynamic segment is added to the second argument in the `link-to` helper. In this recipe, we'll create a `students` route with a dynamic segment.

1. Run this command from the project root to create `resource` for `students`:

    ```
    $ ember g resource students
    ```

    This will create the model, route, and templates needed for our new `students` route.

2. Next, we'll need to update the `router.js` file and add a simple dynamic segment:

    ```
    // app/router.js
    import Ember from 'ember';
    import config from './config/environment';

    var Router = Ember.Router.extend({
      location: config.locationType
    });

    Router.map(function() {
      this.route('students',{path: '/students/:student_id'});
    });

    export default Router;
    ```

    The most important thing to realize here is the path. This is called a dynamic segment and is represented by `:student_id`. By convention, the `students` route will retrieve information from the student model. If the user navigates to `/students/5`, the route will retrieve the student model with the ID of 5. Look for more information on dynamic segments and routes in the *Chapter 4, Ember Router*.

3. Create a new `application.js` file in the `app/routes` folder. For the sake of simplicity, we'll have the application route return an array of student objects that we can then retrieve in our template:

    ```
    // app/routes/application.js

    import Ember from 'ember';

    export default Ember.Route.extend({
      model(){
        return [{id: 1,name: 'Erik Hanchett', age: 16,
          location: 'Reno'},{id: 2,name: 'Jeff Smith', age: 17,
          location: 'San Francisco'},{id: 3,name: 'Kate Smith',
          age: 19, location: 'Sparks'}];
      }
    });
    ```

The `application` route is on top and is inherited by all other routes. For this example, we returned a list of objects with a number of properties. This model will be able to be accessed in our students template.

4. Update the students template in the `app/templates` folder:

```
// app/templates/students.hbs
Student Route<br>
{{model.name}}<br>
{{model.age}}<br>
{{model.location}}<br>
```

This template will display `name`, `age`, and `location` of the model passed to it. Make sure to prefix all the values with `model`.

5. We'll then update the `application.hbs` file with a `{{each}}` helper and `link-to`:

```
// app/templates/application.hbs
<h2 id="title">Welcome to Ember</h2><br>
<br>
{{#each model as |student|}}
   {{#link-to 'students' student}}{{student.name}}
     {{/link-to}} <br>
{{/each}}
{{outlet}}
<br>
<br>
```

In this example, we have an `each` helper that iterates through the model. The `link-to` helper has two arguments. The first is the route, which is `students`. The second is the dynamic segment, `student`. Ember will replace each segment with the value of the corresponding object ID's property. If, for some reason, no model exists, you can explicitly set the value instead:

```
{{#link-to 'students' 1}}Some Student{{/link-to}}
```

This will link the student's route with a dynamic segment with an ID of `1`.

Multiple segments

There might be times where you have nested routes with multiple segments. For example, a blog might have blog posts and each blog post might have comments. In this case, you can specify multiple segments in the `link-to` helper. All you need to do is separate them with a space. For instance, a blog with multiple comments might look like `{{#link-to 'blog.comment' 1 comment}}Comment{{/link-to}}`. The `1` is the first dynamic segment and the comment is the second dynamic segment.

6. After being rendered, three links will be displayed as follows:

```
<a href="/students/1">Erik Hanchett</a>
<a href="/students/2">Jeff Smith</a>
<a href="/students/3">Kate Smith</a>
```

7. Clicking on any link will navigate to the student's route with that ID. The template will then display the student's information on the screen as follows:

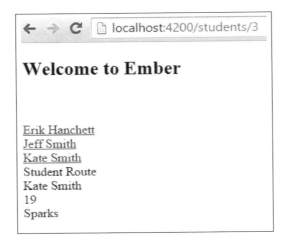

How it works...

The `link-to` helper is used by the templating engine to route a customer throughout an application. It's only used for internal links, not external.

The `link-to` helper takes two or more arguments. The first is the name of the route. The second is used for dynamic segments.

Handling HTML actions

Often, in an application, we'll need to allow interaction with controls that affect the application state. To accomplish this, we'll use actions.

How to do it...

The `{{action}}` helper is used on HTML elements to send actions back to the template's corresponding controller or component when the user clicks on an element. Let's take a look at an example of this.

1. Create a new project, navigate to the root of the `application` directory, and type this command to generate a new component:

   ```
   $ ember g component action-component
   ```

   Keep in mind that all components must have a dash in their names. This will generate the component template, JavaScript files, and test files.

2. Edit the `action-component.js` file in the `components` folder. We'll add the action, `toggleText`:

   ```javascript
   // app/components/action-component.js
   import Ember from 'ember';

   export default Ember.Component.extend({
     showText: true,
     actions: {
       toggleText(){
         this.toggleProperty('showText');
       }
     }
   });
   ```

   In this example, we have a `showText` property that's defaulted to `true`. When the action, `toggleText`, is triggered, it toggles the `showText` property. The `toggleProperty` method sets the opposite value of its current property.

3. The `toggleText` action is now ready to be added to the template. The next step is to add the action to the component template using the `{{action}}` helper:

   ```handlebars
   // app/templates/components/action-component.hbs
   {{#if showText}}
   Lorem ipsum dolor sit amet, consectetur adipiscing elit. Aenean
   dui est, auctor sit amet augue vel, mattis maximus libero.
   Praesent feugiat ex justo, vitae convallis nulla venenatis quis.
   {{/if}}<br>
   <button {{action 'toggleText'}}>{{if showText 'Hide Text' 'Show
   Text'}}</button>
   {{yield}}
   ```

The `if` helper will display text only if the `showText` property is `true`. The button at the bottom has an action called `toggleText` attached to it. Whenever this button is pressed, the `toggleText` action will be invoked by the corresponding `action-component` component. To keep things clear, the button text will show `Hide Text` if the text is shown and `Show Text` if it's hidden.

The `action` helper can be added to any HTML element. As soon as the element is clicked, the action will be triggered.

4. It's good to know that you can attach an action to any HTML element but not all will respond. Some browsers may ignore the click event. In this case, you can use this `css` trick as a workaround:

```
[data-ember-action] {
  cursor: pointer;
}
```

Specifying the type of event

By default, all actions listen for click events. When a click occurs, that action is triggered in the context, component, or controller. You can specify an alternative to the click event with the `on` option. For example, a button with a double-click action would look like `<button {{action 'toggleText' on='doubleClick'}}Show Text</button>`. All event names must be camel-cased and lowercase when assigned to `on`.

5. We now need to add the component to the `application` template file so that it can be displayed:

```
// app/templates/application.hbs
<h2 id="title">Welcome to Ember</h2>
<br>
<br>
{{action-component}}
{{outlet}}
<br>
```

This will add our action component to our `application` template.

6. After loading the application with the Ember server, it will look as follows:

Pressing the **Hide Text** button will hide the text. Pressing it again will show the text.

Allowing modifier keys

By default, the `action` helper will ignore click events when modifier keys such as *Alt* or *Ctrl* are pressed at the same time. If needed, you can specify an `allowedKeys` option. For example, a button with an allowed key *Alt* would look like `<button {{action 'toggleText' allowedKeys='alt'}}Show Text</button>`.

Adding a parameter to an action event

You can have arguments in an action handler that will be passed back to the context. Anything after the action name of the `action` helper will be passed as an argument to the component or controller.

1. To begin, we'll create a new component. After the project is created, run this command in the root of the `project` folder:

```
$ ember g component param-component
```

This will generate the necessary component files for our new `param-component`.

2. Edit the `param-component.js` file and add a new action called `pressed`:

```
// app/components/param-component.js
import Ember from 'ember';

export default Ember.Component.extend({
  actions: {
    pressed(text){
      alert(text);
    }
  }
});
```

In this simple example, the `pressed` action has only one parameter. When the action is triggered, an `alert` box is displayed with the passed in parameter text.

3. The next step is to edit the template and add the action:

```
// app/templates/components/param-component.hbs
{{input text='text' value=hello}}
<button {{action 'pressed' hello}}>Press Me</button>
{{yield}}
```

In this template, we have an `input` helper. The `input` helper will be discussed in more detail in the *Using template input helpers* recipe. The button press triggers the `pressed` action and passes the `hello` text from the input helper to the action.

Allowing default browser action

The action helper, by default, prevents the default browser action of the DOM event. In other words, when a user clicks on a link or button that might otherwise reload the page, Ember prevents this. If needed, you can turn this behavior off using `preventDefault=false`. For example, we can add an action event to a link and have it redirected to a page as well as trigger an event `<a href="thispage.htm" {{action 'pressed' preventDefault=false}}>Press Me</a>`.

4. The next step is to add `param-component` to the application:

```
// app/templates/application.hbs
<h2 id="title">Welcome to Ember</h2>
<br>
<br>
{{param-component}}

{{outlet}}
<br>
```

In this code, we added `param-component` to the `application` template.

5. After starting the server, a textbox will be displayed. Pressing the **Press Me** button will display the text in an alert box. It should look as follows:

6. In some cases, we may not be using an `input` helper. Let's say that we want to have an action event trigger `onblur`. We can specify a `value` option in our `action` helper:

```
// app/templates/components/param-component.hbs
<input type="text" value={{hello}} onblur={{action
  'pressed' value='target.value'}} />
```

The input `text` field has `value` equal to the `hello` property. The `onblur` event is raised whenever the element loses focus. By default, the action handler receives the first parameter of the event listener. In this case, it would be `Event {}`. We must specify the `value` option to specify the target value using `target.value`.

Unfortunately, due to the way Ember binds values, we cannot simply just send the `hello` property as a parameter to the action. This is why we must use the `value` option.

You can test this by entering text in the textbox and clicking outside the box so that it loses focus. It should show the correct text in the alert popup.

How it works...

The `action` helper attaches to HTML elements in order to allow user interaction. It sends named events to the template's corresponding context, component, or controller.

The `action` helper by default sends the first parameter of the event listener. You can send any parameter that you want after the `action` event. If needed, you can specify the `value` option and use `value.target`, which will send the target of the event.

Using template input helpers

To create common form controls, `input` helpers can be used. This recipe will go over how to use them in our Ember applications.

How to do it...

The most common `input` helper is `{{input}}`. It wraps around the `Ember.TextField` view and is almost identical to the traditional `<input>` HTML element.

1. Create a new project. In the `app/templates` folder, open the `application.hbs` file and add an `input` helper:

```
// app/templates/application.hbs
<h2 id="title">Welcome to Ember</h2>
<br>
<br>
{{input value='Hello World'}}
```

This `input` helper is very simple; all it does is set the value of the textbox to `hello world`. It is surrounded by double curly braces and supports the normal input attributes.

2. When rendered, it will look as follows:

```
<h2 id="title">Welcome to Ember</h2>
<br>
<br>
<input type="text" value="Hello World"/>
```

If needed, we can assign properties to the `input` helper.

3. Create a new `application` controller. Run this command in the root `application` folder:

```
$ ember g controller application
```

This will generate a new controller that the application can access.

4. Open the controller and add a new property. We'll call this `helloText`:

```
// app/controllers/application.js
import Ember from 'ember';

export default Ember.Controller.extend({
    helloText: 'Hello World'
});
```

5. Edit the `application.hbs` file again and set `value` to the property:

```
// app/templates/application.hbs
<h2 id="title">Welcome to Ember</h2>
<br>
<br>
{{input value=helloText}}
```

The `helloText` property is now bound to the input value. Attributes that have quoted values will be set directly to the element. If left unquoted, these values will be bound to the property on the template's current rendering context. In this case, this is the controller.

6. Let's add a simple action to the `input` helper. This can be done using the dasherized event name as an attribute to the `input` helper:

```
// app/templates/application.hbs
<h2 id="title">Welcome to Ember</h2>
<br>
<br>
{{input value=helloText key-press='pressed'}}
```

Whenever a key is pressed, the action pressed will be triggered in the component or controller.

7. As we haven't created a key press, we'll add it to our controller:

```
// app/controllers/application.js
...
  actions: {
    pressed(){
      console.log('pressed');
    }
  }
```

Whenever a key is pressed in the textbox, a message will be logged to the console.

How to use checkbox helpers

In the previous example, we created a simple input textbox. We can also create a checkbox in the same way. This uses the `Ember.Checkbox` view.

1. In a new project, open the `application.hbs` file in the `app/templates` folder. Let's add a new checkbox:

```
// app/templates/application.hbs
<h2 id="title">Welcome to Ember</h2>
<br>
<br>
{{input type='checkbox' checked=isChecked}}
```

This is very similar to the input textbox.

2. Generate an `application` controller. This will be used to store our `isChecked` property:

    $ ember g controller application

3. Update the controller with the new `isChecked` property. Set it to `true`:

```
// app/controllers/application.js
import Ember from 'ember';

export default Ember.Controller.extend({
    isChecked: true
});
```

This controller has only a Boolean property, `isChecked`.

4. The `isChecked` property is bound to the checkbox. After it's rendered, it should look as follows:

```
...
<input type="checkbox" checked="true"/>
```

How to use text areas

To create a `textarea` element, we can use the `textarea` helper. This wraps the `Ember.TextArea` view.

Create a new project and edit the `application.hbs` file in the `app/templates` folder. Add a `textarea` helper:

```
// app/templates/application.hbs
<h2 id="title">Welcome to Ember</h2>
<br>
<br>
{{textarea value='hello world' cols='20' rows='10'}}
```

The text area box will be displayed with `20` columns and `10` rows. It will look like this after being rendered:

```
...
<textarea rows="6" cols="80">Hello World</textarea>
```

Adding actions and attributes work in the same way as the `input` and `checkbox` helpers.

How it works...

The input, textarea, and checkbox are all helpers that make it easier to work with common form controls. They wrap around `Ember.TextField`, `Ember.Checkbox`, and `Ember.TextArea`.

With these helpers, we can easily bind elements and actions to them.

Using development helpers

Debugging your template is a task that you'll often use. Here are the steps to do this.

How to do it...

The most basic way of debugging Ember templates is to use `{{log}}` and `{{debugger}}`.

1. Create a new Ember application. Create a new component called `log-example`. Run this command in the root `application` folder:

   ```
   $ ember g component log-example
   ```

   This will create a new component template and JavaScript files.

2. Open the `log-example.js` file in the `app/components` folder and a new property called `helloText`:

   ```
   // app/components/log-example.js
   import Ember from 'ember';

   export default Ember.Component.extend({
       helloText: 'Hello World'
   });
   ```

   This is a simple component with just one property.

3. Open the `log-example.hbs` file in the `app/templates/components` directory. Add `log` to it:

   ```
   // app/templates/components/log-example.hbs
   {{log 'Hello text is' helloText}}
   ```

   This will display a string in the browser's console window.

4. Now we can add this new component to our `application.hbs` file:

   ```
   // app/templates/application.hbs
   <h2 id="title">Welcome to Ember</h2>
   <br>
   <br>
   {{log-example}}
   ```

   After being rendered, the text **Hello text is Hello World** will be displayed in the console.

5. In this same example, let's add `{{debugger}}`. Edit the `log-example.hbs` file and add it at the bottom:

   ```
   // app/templates/components/log-example.hbs
   {{log 'Hello text is' helloText}}
   {{debugger}}
   hi
   ```

The debugger is the equivalent of JavaScript's debugger keyword. It will halt the execution of code and allow the inspection of the current rendering context.

6. If we start the server and load the web page, the browser will halt on the debug statement while loading. At this point, we can open the browser's console window and use the `get` function to find the current value of `helloText`:

```
> get('helloText')
```

```
> "Hello World"
```

The `get` command can retrieve any value from the context. In other words, it can retrieve any value from the component or controller. This works the same if the debug statement was in a `{{each}}` loop.

7. You can get the context of the view as well in the console debugger:

```
> context
```

Ember Inspector

The Ember Inspector is a plugin for Chrome and Firefox web browsers. It makes it easy to debug and understand your Ember application. When you are using the plugin, you can see all sorts of information on your application, including routes, models, templates, controllers, and components. You can download it from the Firefox or Chrome plugin store for free.

How it works...

The Handlebars library has made it easy to debug your templates. They are helpers that interact with the web browser to log information to the console or stop the execution of it.

The Ember's `{{debugger}}` equivalent in JavaScript is the debugger. Both work very much in the same way.

4
Ember Router

In this chapter, we will cover the following recipes:

- ▸ Defining an application route
- ▸ Setting up a route model
- ▸ Handling dynamic segments inside routes
- ▸ Defining routes with templates
- ▸ Using redirection with routes
- ▸ Working with asynchronous routing
- ▸ Loading and error handling
- ▸ Using query parameters

Introduction

The router in Ember is responsible for changing the state of the application when a user performs an action. This can be anything from the user changing the URL to hitting the back button in the application. Regardless of what action is performed, the route handler is responsible. It takes the current URL and maps it to the correct route so that it can be displayed to the user.

Route handlers take care of rendering templates, loading up the model, and redirecting and transitioning from one route to another. They can also handle actions that occur when the model changes.

Defining an application route

When loading your application, the router looks at the URL and matches it to the route. We'll go over some basics on how this works.

How to do it...

The route map is used to define the URL mappings. Let's take a look at adding a new route using this.route.

1. In a new application, open the router.js file in the app folder. To begin, we'll create a new route called about:

```
// app/router.js
import Ember from 'ember';
import config from './config/environment';

var Router = Ember.Router.extend({
  location: config.locationType
});

Router.map(function() {
  this.route('about');
});

export default Router;
```

Router.map in the preceding code handles the routing of the program. The this.route creates the about route. By default, the name of the route will be the same as the path to it. For example, the about route path would be located at /about. We can specifically set the path using path.

2. Instead of having all requests go to /about, let's change the path so that they go to /me:

```
// app/router.js
...
this.route('about',{ path: '/aboutme' });
...
```

The new route about will be mapped to the URL /aboutme now.

3. To test this, we can create a new template and add a `link-to` helper to our application route. First, we'll create the template:

    ```
    $ ember g template about
    ```

    The Ember CLI generated will create the template for us. This will create the `about.hbs` file in the `app/templates` folder.

4. Add the `link-to` helper to the `application.hbs` file:

    ```
    // app/templates/about.hbs
    <h2 id="title">Welcome to Ember</h2>

    {{outlet}}

    {{#link-to 'about'}}about template{{/link-to}}
    ```

    The code creates a new link to the `about` template in the main application template.

5. Add a new message to the `about` template that we just created:

    ```
    // app/templates/about.hbs
    <br>Hello from the about route!<br>
    ```

    This text will be displayed only when we navigate to this new route.

6. We can now run the server and check the output. Run `ember server` and click on the **about template** link. The about route will load and will look as follows:

Application route

When your app first boots up, the application route is loaded. Just like any other route, the application template will load by default. The application route is given for free and does not need to be added to the `app/router.js` file. The `{{outlet}}` will be used to render all other routes. It's a good idea to put the header, footer, and other decorative content here.

Working with nested routes in your application

At times, you may need multiple levels of routes. You might need templates within other templates. This can be accomplished using nested routes.

1. Let's say that we had `about` with a nested `location` and `job` route:

```
// app/router.js
import Ember from 'ember';
import config from './config/environment';

var Router = Ember.Router.extend({
  location: config.locationType
});

Router.map(function() {
  this.route('about', function() {
    this.route('location');
    this.route('job');
  });
});

export default Router;
```

2. The router `map` has the highest-level route called `about`. Underneath this route is the `location` and `job`. Create two templates needed for `location` and `job`:

   $ ember g template about/location

   $ ember g template about/job

   $ ember g template about

   This will create the correct `location.hbs` and `job.hbs` files in the `app/templates/about` folder as well as the `about.hbs` file in the `app/templates` folder.

3. For us to be able to access nested routes, we'll need to edit `about.hbs` and add `outlet` for the `location` and `job` nested routes:

```
// app/templates/about.hbs
<br>Hello from the about route<br>
{{#link-to 'about.location'}}location{{/link-to}}<br>
{{#link-to 'about.job'}}job{{/link-to}}
<br>{{outlet}}<br>
```

   Note how the `link-to` helpers route to `about.location`. You can link nested routes with the dot notation. The `location` and `job` nested routes will render in `{{outlet}}`.

4. Just to make things interesting, we'll update the `job` and `location` route templates:

```
// app/templates/about/location.hbs
Hello from about/location route


// app/templates/about/job.hbs
Hi from the about/job route
```

5. Finally, we'll add a `link-to` helper to the application route:

```
// app/templates/application.hbs
<br>
<br>

{{#link-to 'about'}}Hello{{/link-to}}
{{outlet}}
```

The `link-to` helper will route to about. This will be rendered in `outlet`.

6. After running `ember server`, you'll have access to click on the links and go between the routes. It should look similar to the following image:

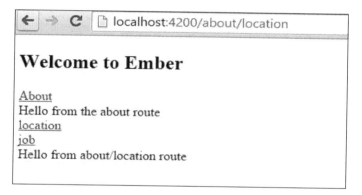

If we click on the **job** link, the URL changes to `http://localhost:4200/about/job`. The `{{outlet}}` in the `about` template will then display the `job` template information.

Adding a wildcard

You can use wildcards in your routes. This allows you to create URLs that match multiple segments. Let's create a wildcard for any URL that isn't found.

1. In a new project, update the `router.js` file in the `app` folder:

```
// app/router.js
import Ember from 'ember';
import config from './config/environment';

var Router = Ember.Router.extend({
  location: config.locationType
});

Router.map(function() {
    this.route('page-not-found', {path: '/*wildcard' });
});

export default Router;
```

The `/*wildcard` path will catch all the undefined routes and route them to `page-not-found`.

2. Create a new `page-not-found` template:

```
$ ember g template page-not-found
```

```
// app/templates/page-not-found
<br>Not Found</br>
```

This route will render in the `application.hbs` outlet whenever a user navigates to a URL that matches `/*` and no existing routes match.

Adding dynamic segments to our about application

One important responsibility of the route is to load a model. In this example, we'll create a simple dynamic segment in the router that lists multiple jobs for the about route.

1. In a new project, edit the `router.js` file and add the following code:

```
// app/router.js
import Ember from 'ember';
import config from './config/environment';
```

```
var Router = Ember.Router.extend({
  location: config.locationType
});


Router.map(function() {
    this.route('about', function(){
        this.route('location', {path: '/about/:location_id'});
    });
});


export default Router;
```

2. View the output, and we can see that the router map shows an `about` route and a nested `location` route below it. The `location` route is a dynamic segment that starts with `:` and is followed by an identifier. The `:location_id` identifier will retrieve the model information from the `location` model.

   For example, if a user navigates to `/about/5`, the route will set `location_id` of 5 so that the `location` model with the ID of 5 is loaded. We'll be going over the `about` routes in more detail in the next section.

Index routes

At every level of nesting, including the application layer, Ember.js automatically creates a route called **index**. You don't need to map this in `router.js`. Similar to the application route, it's already there. The index route will automatically be rendered in the outlet of its parent's template. For example, if you created an `index.hbs` file in the `app/templates` folder, it would automatically be rendered in the `application.hbs` outlet. Keep this in mind when you create routes.

How it works...

Routes in Ember.js are defined in the `app/router.js` file. The router map is used to define each route, and it tells the Ember application what path should be used in the URL. By convention, each route has a corresponding template with the same name. Wildcards and dynamic segments can make routes more versatile so that they can load specific data.

Setting up a route model

Occasionally, you'll need to retrieve data from a model for a template. The route is responsible for loading the appropriate model. This recipe will go over how to do this.

How to do it...

1. In a new application, open the `router.js` file and add a new route. We'll call this route `students`:

```
// app/router.js
import Ember from 'ember';
import config from './config/environment';

var Router = Ember.Router.extend({
  location: config.locationType
});

Router.map(function() {
  this.route('students');
});

export default Router;
```

The `students` route will retrieve data from the `students` route handler.

2. Generate the `students` route. This will create the `students` route handler and template:

```
$ ember g route students
```

3. In the `students.js` file, add a new model that returns a JavaScript object:

```
// app/routes/students.js
import Ember from 'ember';

export default Ember.Route.extend({
    model() {
      return [1,2,3,4,5,6,7];
    }
});
```

The `model` hook normally returns an Ember Data record. However, it can also return any promise objects, plain JavaScript objects, or arrays. Ember will wait until the data is loaded or the promise is resolved before rendering the template.

For simplicity in our example, we returned an array.

4. Create a simple `each` loop in the template to display the data from `model`:

```
// app/templates/students.hbs
{{#each model as |number|}}
    Number: {{number}}<br>
{{/each}}
```

The `each` loop will display each `number` in the array. The model data is returned from the route that we created earlier.

5. Run `ember server` and load the route at `http://localhost:4200/students`. It will look like the following image after it is rendered:

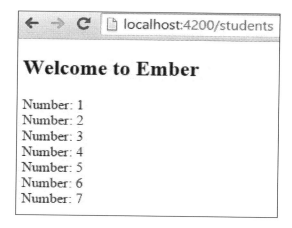

How it works...

A very important job of a route is loading the model. Models are objects that represent data that your application may present to the user. The route can return an Ember Data record, array, or object.

Handling dynamic segments inside routes

Using dynamic segments and dynamic models is an important aspect of routes. The following recipe will go over how this can be accomplished.

Getting ready

Before we begin our recipes, we'll need to set up a plugin called **Ember CLI Mirage**. Ember plugins, also known as **add-ons**, make it easy to share common code between applications. The Ember CLI Mirage plugin makes it easy to create a mock server so that we can develop, test, and prototype our data. We won't cover too much of this add-on in this chapter. If you'd like more information, you can download it at `https://github.com/samselikoff/ember-cli-mirage`.

In this example, we'll use the **Ember Data's RESTAdapter**, not the new **JSON API** adapter.

1. In a new project, run this installation command in the `application` folder:

   ```
   $ ember install ember-cli-mirage@0.1.11
   ```

   This will install version `0.1.11` of Ember CLI Mirage, Bower, and `npm` packages in the application. We'll be using this version for all the examples in the book.

2. Open the `config.js` file in the `app/mirage` folder. Add a couple of new routes:

   ```
   // app/mirage/config.js
   export default function() {

   this.get('/students');
   this.get('/students/:id');
   }
   ```

   The first fake route, `/students`, will return all the student data from our Mirage in the memory database. The second fake route, `/students/:id`, will return only the data that matches the ID in the URL. This will be used later when we try out dynamic segments with our models.

3. Create a new set of fixture data for `students`. Create a new file called `students.js` in the `app/mirage/fixtures` directory:

   ```
   // app/mirage/fixtures/students.js
   export default [
     {id: 1, name: 'Jane Smith', age: 15},
     {id: 2, name: 'Erik Hanchett', age: 14},
     {id: 3, name: 'Suzy Q', age: 17}
   ];
   ```

This file name, `students.js`, matches the route and will be used to load the data in Mirages in the memory database. Be aware that Mirage also supports factories. Factories is an immensely powerful feature that makes it extremely easy to load lots of fake data. The factories can be used in test cases as well.

For simplicity's sake, we'll just use fixture data.

4. Load a new scenario for our application. Update the `app/mirage/scenarios/default.js` file:

```
// app/mirage/scenarios/default.js
export default function( server ) {

    server.loadFixtures();
}
```

The `default.js` file in the `scenarios` folder is used to seed the database in development. The `server.loadFixtures()` method loads all the fixture data so that it can be accessible to the `/students` route.

How to do it...

Data in our model may never change. On the other hand, that data might change many times depending on interactions with the user. This recipe will cover how to use dynamic segments with your routes and return data from the model.

1. Begin by creating a new resource called `students`. Then generate an adapter named `application` and finally, a route:

```
$ ember g resource students
$ ember g adapter application
$ ember g route application
```

This will generate the routes, adapter, and template files needed for this recipe. Keep in mind that by generating the `application` route, you will be prompted to overwrite the `application.hbs` file. You can select *n*, for no, when this occurs.

2. Update the `router.js` file with the new dynamic segment route:

```
// app/router.js
import Ember from 'ember';
import config from './config/environment';

var Router = Ember.Router.extend({
  location: config.locationType
});
```

```
Router.map(function() {
  this.route('students',  {path: '/students/:student_id'});
});
```

```
export default Router;
```

This new route has a path of `/students/:student_id`. This route will extract `:student_id` from the URL and pass it to the model hook as the first argument.

For example, let's say that we have a list of `students` and we wanted to be able to access each student's data by visiting `/students/1` and `/students/2`. Each URL would then return the data for that student.

3. Update the `application.js` file in the `app/adapters` folder:

```
import DS from 'ember-data';
```

```
export default DS.RESTAdapter.extend({
});
```

This will create a new `RESTAdapter` that Ember will use for this example. This will be covered more in the models chapter.

4. Edit the `students.js` file in the `app/models` folder. This file is our model and will be used to retrieve data from the Mirage mock server that we created earlier:

```
// app/models/student.js
import DS from 'ember-data';

export default DS.Model.extend({
    name: DS.attr('string'),
    age: DS.attr('number')

});
```

This creates a new model with two attributes, `name` and `age`. The model file defines what the data will look like. We'll be covering this more in the *Chapter 7, Ember Models and Ember Data*. For now, we will be retrieving this data from the mock server.

5. Update the `students.js` file in the `app/routes` folder. Add the Ember Data `findRecord` method:

```
// app/routes/students.js
import Ember from 'ember';

export default Ember.Route.extend({
    model(param) {
        return this.store.findRecord('student',param.student_id);
    }
});
```

The `model` hook here has one argument, `param`. The `param` argument is `student_id` that is passed from the route's URL. Ember Data has a `findRecord` method that takes two parameters. The first parameter is the name of the model and the second is the ID.

This model will return the student record with the ID passed to it. We can now use this in our template.

6. Edit the `students.hbs` file in the `app/templates` folder. Add the model information:

```
// app/templates/students.hbs
{{model.name}}
{{model.age}}
```

The `{{model.name}}` and `{{model.age}}` properties will retrieve the model information passed to the template from the route.

At this point, we should be able to run `ember server` and see data when we access `http://localhost:4200/students/1`. To make things a little easier, we'll go ahead and create a new route handler for the main application route.

7. Edit the `application.js` file in the `app/routes` folder:

```
// app/routes/application.js
import Ember from 'ember';

export default Ember.Route.extend({
    model() {
      return this.store.findAll('student');
    }
});
```

Multiple models

At times, you may want to use multiple models in one route. This can be accomplished using `Ember.RSVP.hash`. The hash takes parameters that return promises. When all the parameters are resolved, then `Ember.RSVP.hash` is resolved. In the model, it may look like this: return `Ember.RSVP.hash({ students: this.store.findAll('student'), books: this.store.findAll('book') })`. Each model is separated by a comma.

This will allow our application to retrieve all the records from our student model.

8. Open the `application.hbs` file in the `app/templates` folder. We'll add an `each` iterator that will link to each student's information:

```
// app/templates/application.hbs
<h2 id="title">Welcome to Chapter 4</h2>

{{#each model as |student|}}
    {{#link-to 'students' student.id}}{{student.name}}
      {{/link-to}}<br>
{{/each}}

{{outlet}}
```

In this template, we are iterating through all the records in the `student` model. We are using each individual student's name as a link to our dynamic segment. The `student.id` argument is passed to the `link-to` helper.

9. After starting the server, you'll see a list of the students and a link to each student's information. After clicking on the student's name, the `student.hbs` template will load with the student's information. It will look like the following image:

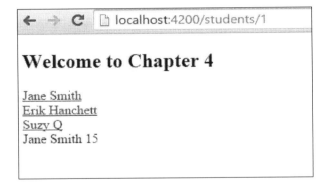

How it works...

Dynamic models allow data to change depending on the user action. This data will depend on the dynamic segment setup in the `router.js` file. The segment is defined in the `router` file and passed from the URL to the model hook as its first argument. Ember Data uses the `findRecord` method to find the correct record and return it to the template so that it's available for use.

Defining routes with templates

Another job of the route handler is rendering the appropriate template. Here is a recipe that goes over this.

How to do it...

In this recipe, we'll create a few nested routes and check where they get rendered.

1. In a new project, create a new `students` and `schools` route:

    ```
    $ ember g route schools
    $ ember g route schools/students
    ```

    This will create the nested `students` and `schools` route.

2. Let's take a look at the `router.js` file:

    ```
    // app/router.js
    import Ember from 'ember';
    import config from './config/environment';

    var Router = Ember.Router.extend({
      location: config.locationType
    });

    Router.map(function() {
      this.route('schools', {}, function() {
        this.route('students', {});
      });
    });

    export default Router;
    ```

    The generated command already created the routes that we need. The `schools` route has a nested route called `students`.

    By convention, the route will render the template with the same name. Therefore, the `schools` route will render to the `schools.hbs` file while the `students` route will be rendered to the `schools/students.hbs` file.

3. Update the `schools.hbs` file:

```
// app/templates/schools.hbs
This is the school route<br>
{{outlet}}
```

The `{{outlet}}` will render the `students.hbs` file in the `schools` folder. Every template will be rendered to `{{outlet}}` of its parent route's template.

4. Update the `students.hbs` file in the `app/templates/schools` folder:

```
// app/templates/schools/students.hbs
This is the students route<br>
{{outlet}}
```

5. Run `ember server` and you should see this result:

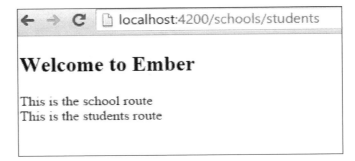

6. By visiting `http://localhost:4200/schools/students`, both the templates are displayed. The application `{{outlet}}` renders the school template. The school template's `{{outlet}}` renders the students template.

7. If required, you can change where the route renders. Instead of rendering in the template with the same name, you can set it to anything using the `renderTemplate()` method in the route handler:

```
// app/routes/school.js
import Ember from 'ember';

export default Ember.Route.extend({
  renderTemplate() {
    this.render('anotherSchool');
  }
});
```

The school route will now render to the `anotherSchool` template.

How it works...

Routes, by default, will render a template based on the same name as the route. Ember does this by convention. On the other hand, using `renderTemplate` in the route handler can change this default. This is all done under the hood by the Ember API.

Using redirection with routes

A very important feature of routes is redirection. This recipe will go over using the `transitionTo` method.

How to do it...

In our route handler, we have special hooks called `beforeModel` and `afterModel`. We can use these hooks to perform actions before the model is loaded or after the model is loaded. The `transitionTo` method can be used to redirect the application to different routes.

1. In a new application, create a new `students` route:

   ```
   $ ember g route students
   ```

   This will generate the `students` route and template files.

2. For the sake of simplicity, we'll have the route handler return a simple array of numbers:

   ```
   // app/routes/students.js
   import Ember from 'ember';

   export default Ember.Route.extend({
       model() {
         return [1,2,3,4,5,6,7,8,9];
       }
   });
   ```

3. Edit the `routes/students.js` file again. This time, we'll add a before hook and a transition to it:

   ```
   // app/routes/students.js
   ...
   beforeModel(){
     this.transitionTo('teachers');
   }
   ```

   The `transitionTo` method will redirect from one route to another. This option will redirect before the model is loaded and transition to the teacher's route.

4. We can also transition after the model is loaded using the `afterModel()` hook:

```
// app/routes/students.js
...
afterModel(){
  this.transitionTo('teachers');
}
```

This will wait until the model is fully loaded before transitioning to the new route. You can check the loaded route before transitioning, if needed.

Redirect

When transitioning to nested routes, it's a good idea to use the `redirect` method instead of the `afterModel` or `beforeModel` hooks. This will prevent `beforeModel`, `afterModel`, and `model` from firing again after redirecting. Keep this in mind when dealing with `transitionTo` in nested routes.

How it works...

The `afterModel` and `beforeModel` hooks occur after or before a model is loaded. The `transitionTo` method is used to redirect from one route to another. It can be used in the route handler or anywhere else in the application.

Working with asynchronous routing

A more advanced feature of the router is dealing with asynchronous logic. The following recipes explain this concept using promises.

How to do it...

In the route, Ember makes heavy use of promises. Promises are objects that represent an eventual value. We can use promises in our model.

1. Create a new router for the application route:

```
$ ember g route application
```

If prompted to overwrite the template, type Y. This will generate the router file for the default application route.

2. Add a new model to the `application.js` file in the `app/router` folder:

```
// app/router/application.js
import Ember from 'ember';

export default Ember.Route.extend({
    model() {
        return  new Ember.RSVP.Promise(function(resolve) {
            resolve({message: 'Resolved'});
        });
    },
    setupController(controller, model){
        this._super(controller, model);
        console.log(model.message);
    }
});
```

In the router, we created a new model. This model will be accessible to our application template. In this model, we are returning `Ember.RSVP.Promise`, which is Ember's way of dealing with a promise. It can either resolve or reject. For the sake of simplicity, we are having it return a message.

The `setupController` hook to set up the controller for the current route. As we are overwriting `setupController`, it also overwrites its default behavior. Therefore, we must call `super` on it. Otherwise it may effect how it normally behaves. We can use `console.log` to output the model message to the console.

Asynchronous routing

During a transition, the model hook is fired in the router. If, during this transition, the model is returning an array, it will return immediately. On the other hand, if the model is returning a promise, it must wait for this promise to fulfill or reject. The router will consider any object with a `then` method defined on it to be a promise. After the promise fulfills, the transition will continue from where it left off. It's possible to chain multiple promises, so the next promise or model must be fulfilled before the transition will be complete.

3. Let's edit the application router one more time and set it to reject:

```
// app/routes/application.js
import Ember from 'ember';

export default Ember.Route.extend({
    model() {
        return Ember.RSVP.Promise.reject('error');
    },
```

```
setupController(controller, model)
    this._super(controller, model);
    console.log(model.message);
},
actions: {
    error(reason){
        console.log(reason);
    }
}
});
```

In the preceding code, the model returns a rejected promise. As described in the *Loading and error handling* recipe, there is something called an `error` event. This will fire only when an error occurs in the model. We can then log the error to the console.

4. We can test this by editing the `application.hbs` file in the `app/templates` folder:

```
// app/templates/application.hbs
{{outlet}}

Message: {{model.message}}
```

If the promise doesn't reject, the model message will be displayed. If the model rejects, then nothing will be displayed; the route halts the loading and the console will show the message, **error**.

Error events bubble upwards. In this case, we are already on the application route and it can't bubble up any further. If we were in another route, we could have returned true and that error would have bubbled up to the application error event.

5. Edit the `application.js` file again in the `app/router` folder. Let's deal with the rejection:

```
// app/routers/application.js
import Ember from 'ember';

export default Ember.Route.extend({
    model() {
        return new Ember.RSVP.Promise(function(resolve,reject) {
            reject('error');
        }).then(null, function() {
            return {message: 'Returned from rejection};
        });
    },
```

```
setupController(controller, model){
  this._super(controller, model);
  console.log(model.message);
},
actions: {
  error(reason){
    console.log(reason);
  }
}

});
```

In the preceding code, the RSVP promise rejects. However, we then return the message anyway, by chaining another promise at the end. This way the transition won't halt and will continue.

6. Run `ember server` and open a web page. You should see this message:

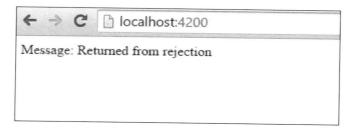

This message shows **Returned from rejection** because we handled the promise reject callback and returned a message anyway.

How it works...

Promises are a way for Ember to handle asynchronous logic. A promise is an object that represents an eventual value. The promise can either reject or fullfil, as in resolve a value. To retrieve the value or handle when it rejects, you can use the then method, which can accept two different callbacks. The first is for fulfillment and the second is for rejection. For example, you might use the rejection to retry or return different data.

Loading and error handling

When routes are loading or there's an error, we have the ability to let the user know what's happening. This recipe will go over the basics on how to do this.

How to do it...

1. In a new project, create a new `students` route:

   ```
   $ ember g route students
   ```

   The `ember generate` command will create all the necessary files for the `students` route.

2. Edit the `students.js` file in the `app/routes` folder. Add a new model to return:

   ```
   // app/routes/students.js
   import Ember from 'ember';

   export default Ember.Route.extend({
       model(){
           return new Ember.RSVP.Promise(function (resolve, reject) {
             Ember.run.later((function() {
               resolve( [1,2,3,4,5,6,7,8,9]);
             }), 2000);
           });
       }
   });
   ```

   In our route file, we are returning an Ember `RSVP` promise. This promise resolves to a simple array that will be returned. `Ember.run.later` is a built-in Ember method that is a part of the Ember run loop. It acts like the JavaScript's `setTimeout()`. In this case, we are setting the timeout for 2,000 milliseconds so that we can simulate what might occur if the model was slow to load. After two seconds pass, the resolve will return with the array.

3. Add a loading substate template in the `app/templates` folder:

   ```
   // app/templates/students-loading.hbs
   <h1> Loading! Please wait! </h1>
   ```

   This substate will be loaded while the students route is loading. A loading substate is created by adding a template with the name of the route and a dash loading at the end. For example, for the students route in our example, we called the `students-loading.hbs` substate. The application loading the substate would be `application-loading.hbs`.

4. As an alternative to substates, we can use a loading event in the route. If the `beforeModel`, `model`, and `afterModel` hooks don't resolve immediately, the loading event will be fired. Add a new loading action that displays an alert box while the model loads and transitions to the application route:

```
// app/routes/students.js
...
    },
    actions: {
      loading(transition, originRoute) {
        alert('Sorry this page is taking so long to load!');
        this.transitionTo('application');
      }
    }
...
```

The alert box will fire while the route is loading.

5. Navigate to `http://localhost:4200/students` and you'll see the alert box while the model is loading.

Creating an error substate

Error substates occur whenever an error is encountered. It's very similar to the loading substate.

1. In a new application, create a `teachers` route:

   ```
   $ ember g route teachers
   ```

   This will create all the necessary files for the `teachers` route.

2. Edit the `teachers.js` file in the `app/routes` folder. Add a new `Ember.RSVP.Promise` with a reject:

```
// app/routes/teachers.js
import Ember from 'ember';

export default Ember.Route.extend({
    model() {
      return new Ember.RSVP.Promise(function (resolve,
        reject) {
        reject('error');
      });
    }
```

In this example, we return a new `Ember.RSVP.Promise` that will reject. This will cause an error to occur.

3. Create a new `teachers-error.hbs` file in the `app/templates` folder. This will be displayed when an error occurs in the `teachers` route:

```
// app/templates/teachers-error.hbs
<h1>Error Loading!</h1>
```

Error substates, like loading substates, must be named after the route with a dash loading at the end. The template will be displayed during an error and doesn't need any other logic to occur.

4. Alternatively, you can also use the error event in the route to display an error and redirect to a different route:

```
// app/routes/teachers.js
...
    },
    actions: {
      error(error, transition) {
        alert('Sorry this page is taking so long to load!');
        this.transitionTo('application');
      }
    }
```

Using the error event is just another way to handle errors. We could certainly have created an error route to transition to.

How it works...

The Ember route has built-in methods and events to handle errors and loading. When loading information, the model hook is waiting for the query to get completed. During this time, a template with the name dash loading at the end will be transitioned to immediately and synchronously. The URL will not be effected. After the query completes, the loading route will be exited and the original route will continue.

When dealing with errors, the error template will be loaded. Once again, the URL will not change to the error route. The error will be passed to the error state as it's model.

Using query parameters

Query parameters allow you to use the URL for the application state. In these recipes, we'll use query parameters in several different ways to show how it works.

How to do it...

Query parameters are optional key-value pairs. They will appear to the right of ? in a URL.

1. In a new project, generate a new `application` controller:

    ```
    $ ember g controller application
    ```

    The `application` controller will be generated in the `app/controllers` folder.

2. Update the application controller with a new `queryParams` for `student`:

    ```
    / app/controllers/application.js
    import Ember from 'ember';

    export default Ember.Controller.extend({
        queryParams: ['student'],
        student: null
    });
    ```

    This will set up the binding between the `student` query parameter in the URL and the `student` property in the controller. If either one changes, the other will change as well.

    If the `student` property was set to anything other than null, then the `student` property will have a default value. This is important to remember because query parameter values are cast to the same datatype as the default value. In other words, if the student property was defaulted to the number *1* and you changed the URL to `/?student=2`, the property would be set to the number 2, not the string `"2"`. Additionally, remember that default values will not be serialized in the URL.

3. Update the `application.hbs` file in the `app/templates` folder. We'll add the `student` property to test:

    ```
    // app/templates/application.hbs
    <h2 id="title">Welcome to Ember</h2>

    {{outlet}}
    student: {{student}}
    ```

    This is a very simple template that just displays the `student` information from the controller.

4. Start Ember server and try changing the URL. Navigate to `http://localhost:4200?students=Erik`. The template will be updated in order to display the new student information:

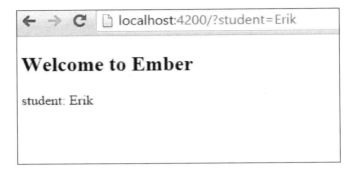

Everything to the right of the question mark ? in the URL can be used in the query parameter. Each parameter is separated by an ampersand. In this case, the student property is set to Erik. This will be updated in the template.

Adding a link-to helper with a query parameter

It's important to realize that we can pass query parameters using the `link-to` helper.

1. In a new project, create a new `application.js` controller:

   ```
   $ ember g controller application
   ```

   This will generate the `application` controller that we can use for our query parameter.

2. Edit the application controller and add a new query parameter:

   ```
   // app/controllers/application.js
   import Ember from 'ember';

   export default Ember.Controller.extend({
       queryParams: ['student'],
       student: null
   });
   ```

   In this example, we created a simple query parameter called `student`.

3. Update the `application.hbs` file in the `app/templates` folder. Add the `student` property and new `link-to` helper with a query parameter:

   ```
   // app/templates/application.hbs
   <h2 id="title">Welcome to Ember</h2>
   ```

```
{{outlet}}
student: {{student}}<br>
{{#link-to 'application' (query-params student='Jane')
  }}Jane Query{{/link-to}}
```

You can add a query parameter to `link-to` by surrounding it with parentheses and using the `query-params` sub-expression helper. After the sub-expression comes the key-value pair. In this case, we have a `student` key.

4. Start Ember server and click on the **Jane Query** link. The following page should appear:

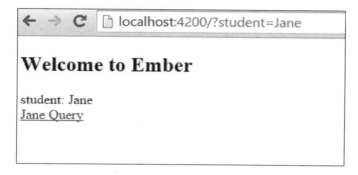

Using TransitionTo with query parameters

Query parameters can be used when transitioning routes with the `transitionTo` method. You can add the query parameter as the final argument with the object key, `queryParmams`. For example, if you need to transition to the application route and you need to pass the query parameter for student, it might look like this:

```
this.transitionTo('application', { queryParams: {
student: 'Erik' }});
```

Resetting a controller's query parameters

By default, query parameters are sticky. In other words, they are preserved when you move in and out of the route. They will also preserve the model loaded in the route.

You can override this behavior in a couple of ways. One is to pass the default query parameter to the `link-to` helper or use `transitionTo`. The other way is to use the `Route.resetController` hook.

1. Create a new project and generate a new route called `route1`:

```
$ ember g route route1
$ ember g controller route1
```

   This will create a new route and controller for `route1`.

2. Edit the `route1.js` file in the `app/controllers` folder:

```
// app/controllers/route1.js
import Ember from 'ember';

export default Ember.Controller.extend({
    queryParams: ['student'],
    student: null,
});
```

   Just like our previous example, we are using a simple query parameter called `student`.

3. Edit the `route1.js` file in the `app/routes` folder. Add a new `resetController` hook to the route:

```
// app/routes/route1.js
import Ember from 'ember';

export default Ember.Route.extend({
    resetController: function
      (controller, isExiting, transition) {
        this._super(controller,isExiting,transition);
        if (isExiting) {
          controller.set('student', null);
        }
    }
});
```

   In this route, we are using the `resetController` hook. This will fire whenever someone exits or transitions from the route. As before, we must call super so that we don't prevent the default behavior. The `isExiting` argument will be false only if the route's model is changing, otherwise it will fire.

   The `controller.set` method is a way in which we can access the student property. We'll set it to null so that when we move away from route1, it will not be preserved.

4. Edit the `application.hbs` file in the `app/templates` folder. Add a `link-to` helper to the new `route1` route:

```
// app/templates/application.hbs
<h2 id="title">Welcome to Ember</h2>
{{#link-to 'route1'}}Route 1{{/link-to}}<br>
{{outlet}}
```

This template is very simple. All we are doing is creating a link to the new `route1`.

5. Edit the `route1.hbs` file in the `app/templates` folder. Add the `student` property and a link back to the main `application` route:

```
Route 1<br>
student: {{student}}<br>
{{#link-to 'application'}}App{{/link-to}}<br>
```

This template displays the `student` property that we can set via query parameters. It then has a link back to the main `application` route.

6. Run `ember server` and load the application. Enter the URL, `http://localhost:4200/route1?student=Erik`. This will display `route1` with the query parameter for student. If you click on the app link, it will bring you back to the main application. If you click on the **Route 1** link again, it will not preserve the query parameter and will be reset. It will look like the following image:

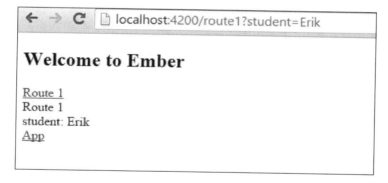

How it works...

Query parameters are key-value pairs that appear to the right of ? in the URL of the application. They help define an additional application state by serializing data in the URL. They are set in the route-driven controllers. We can use `transitionTo` and `link-to` helpers to navigate to them easily.

5

Ember Controllers

In this chapter, we'll cover the following recipes:

- ▸ Storing application properties
- ▸ Handling actions in controllers
- ▸ Working with transitions
- ▸ Managing dependencies between controllers

Introduction

Controllers in Ember.js are similar to components. They can encapsulate code, handle actions, and have properties. In addition, controllers can transition to different parts of the application and retrieve information from other controllers.

In the near future, controllers will be completely replaced by components. However, until this happens, it's good to have some basic understanding on how controllers work.

Storing application properties

One advantage of a controller is storing properties. Controllers have properties that are stored in the application, which is unlike the model where properties are saved to the server. In this recipe, we'll take a look at a few different types of properties and how they can be displayed in a template.

How to do it...

1. In a new application, run the following command:

   ```
   $ ember g controller application
   ```

   In this application, we'll be using the `application controller` to store all our properties.

2. Update the application controller to add a new action and a few properties:

   ```
   // app/controllers/application.js
   import Ember from 'ember';

   export default Ember.Controller.extend({
       prop2: 'test',
       prop3: true,
       actions: {
         enter(val){
           alert(this.get('prop1'));
           alert(this.getProperties('prop1','prop2').prop1);
           alert(val);
           this.toggleProperty('prop3');
         }
       }
   });
   ```

   This controller has two properties. The first property contains a string. The second has a Boolean value of `true` attached to it. The `enter` action displays a few alert boxes. Let's take a closer look at the `enter` action:

   ```
   alert(this.get('prop1'));
   alert(this.getProperties('prop1','prop2').prop1);
   alert(val);
   this.toggleProperty('prop3');
   ```

   When accessing properties in Ember, always use `this.get` and `this.set`. This guarantees that the property will be read or set correctly in Ember. In addition, we can use `this.getProperties`. This allows us to get multiple properties at once. It returns an object of those properties and their values.

   Another useful method is `toggleProperty`. This will take a Boolean value and toggle it. In other words, a value of `false` will become `true` and vice versa.

   Be aware that you don't have to declare each property in the controller definition. Properties can be retrieved directly from the template and be manipulated. In the preceding example, the `prop1` property is retrieved from the template. It was never defined in the controller. If needed, you can set default property values.

3. Update the template for the application. Display the properties:

```
// app/templates/application.hbs
<h2 id="title">Welcome to Ember</h2>

{{outlet}}

<input type='text' value={{prop1}}>One way input<br>
Property 1:{{prop1}}<br>
Property 2:{{prop2}}<br>
{{input type='text'  value=prop1}}Two way input helper<br>
<button {{action 'enter' prop1}}>Value of prop1</button><br>

Propert 3:{{prop3}}
```

The `prop1` property is bound to the bracket input and `input` helper. By default, bracket input tags are one-way. What this means is that the `prop1` property is retrieved from the controller when the template is rendered. It's copied over, and changes to the property are not reflected back in the controller. On the other hand, `input` helpers are bound two-way. Any changes to the value in the `input` helper will be reflected in the controller.

4. Start the Ember server and update the values in the one-way input:

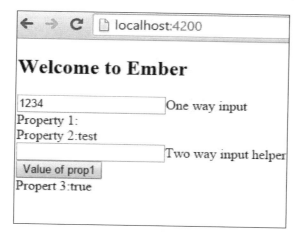

Even though the bracket input tag value is set to `prop1`, it's not changing the `{{prop1}}` property elsewhere in the template. This is because the value is set to work only one way. The only way to change the value of `prop1` in the controller is to send it as an action back to the controller from the template.

This is the basis behind data down, actions up. Data is copied down to the template from the controller or component. Any changes to it are then sent back in an action to the parent component or controller. Keep this concept in mind as it is becoming more and more popular in Ember.

5. Update the values in the two-way input helper box:

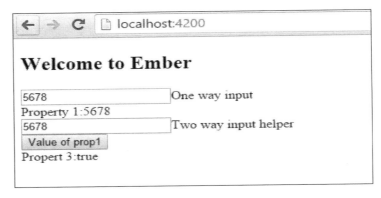

The two-way `input` helper updates all the values in the template because it's linked back to the controller. Any changes to the property in the template are reflected back in the controller because it's two-way bound.

6. Press the **Value of prop1** button:

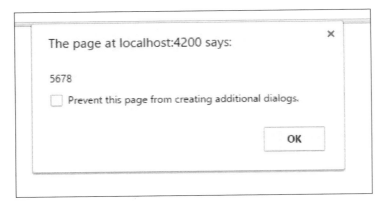

When the button is clicked, an action is triggered. It displays three alert boxes. Each alert box will display the `prop1` property. It will then toggle the third Boolean property from `true` to `false`.

Computed properties, or observers, can be added to controllers as well. To learn more about these, check out *Chapter 2, The Ember.Object Model*.

How it works...

Controllers can use properties to show information to a user. Unlike models, they are not persisted to a server. However, they are persisted in the application state. When working with templates, they can be one-way or two-way bound.

Handling actions in controllers

Actions are important to controllers. They are triggered by the user action and can be used to change the application state. In this recipe, we'll create four different types of actions and see how they react to different situations.

How to do it...

1. In a new application, generate the following files:

```
$ ember g controller application
$ ember g route application
```

   We'll be using the controller and application to store actions. Some actions will bubble up to the route, and some won't.

2. Update the application controller and add three new actions:

```
// app/controllers/application.js
import Ember from 'ember';

export default Ember.Controller.extend({
    actions: {
      action1(){
        alert('Application controller action action1');
      },
      action2(){
        alert('Application controller action action2');
        return true;
      },
      action3(val){
        alert(`Value Passed: ${val}`);
      }
    }
});
```

Let's take a look at each action:

```
action1(){
  alert('Application controller action action1');
},
```

This is a normal action. It just displays an alert box:

```
action2(){
  alert('Application controller action action2');
  return true;
},
```

This action is a little more interesting. By default, all controller actions `return` `false` if they exist in the controller. By returning the value to `true`, this action will bubble up to the `application` route after the alert box is displayed. The route can then handle the action:

```
action3(val){
  alert(`Value Passed: ${val}`);
}
```

The action has a value passed to it. It will display this value to the user in an alert box. The text in the alert box is using something called ES6 template strings. This makes it a little easier to display variables in text.

3. Update the application route with two more actions:

```
// app/routes/application.js
import Ember from 'ember';

export default Ember.Route.extend({
    actions: {
      enter(){
        alert('Application route action enter!');
      },
      action2(){
        alert('Application route action action2!');
      }
    }
});
```

Each action displays an alert box. You might have noticed that the `enter` action was not present in the controller. By convention, template `actions` will look first in the controller. If the action is not defined in the controller, it will bubble up to the route.

4. Add four buttons to the application template:

```
// app/templates/application.hbs
<h2 id="title">Welcome to Ember</h2>

<button {{action 'action1'}}>Action 1 in controller</button>
<button {{action 'action2'}}>
   Action 2 in controller and route</button>
<button {{action 'action3' 'Hello World'}}>
   Action 3 Passing Values</button>
<button {{action 'enter'}}>
   Action enter only in route</button>
```

Each button has an action bound to it. By default, this is bound to the click event; this can be changed if needed.

5. Run ember server. Open a web browser to see the following screen:

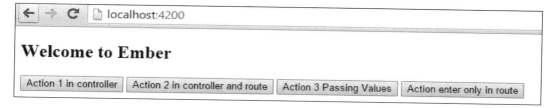

Each button represents a different type of action.

6. Click on the first button:

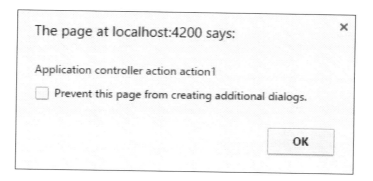

This displays a message from the controller.

7. Click on the second button:

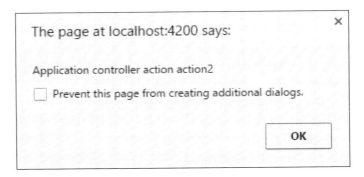

8. This alert box is displayed first from the controller:

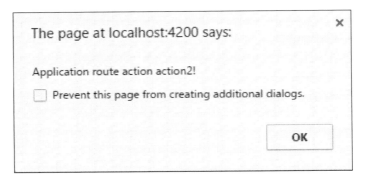

This second alert box is displayed from the application route.

9. Click on the third action:

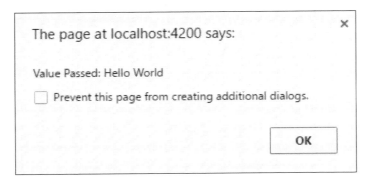

This shows the message from the controller with the value passed.

10. Click on the last button:

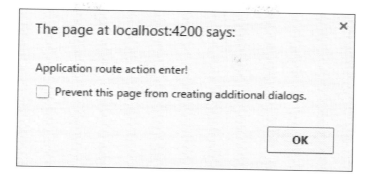

The page at localhost:4200 says:

Application route action enter!

☐ Prevent this page from creating additional dialogs.

OK

This will show the message from the application route as it was not defined in the controller.

How it works...

Actions in Ember bubble up but they are dependent on the user action. They start in the controller and then move to the route. We can add actions to our templates and pass values from the template to our actions.

Working with transitions

When inside a route, you can use the controller to transition to another route. We'll look at an example on how to transition from one route to another.

How to do it...

1. In a new application, generate the following files:

```
$ ember g route foo1
$ ember g route foo2
$ ember g controller foo1
$ ember g controller foo2
$ ember g template index
```

This will generate two different routes for us—the foo1 and foo2 routes. Each route will have a button that transitions to the other route. Each controller will handle the action logic.

2. Add an action to the foo1 controller:

```
// app/controllers/foo1.js
import Ember from 'ember';

export default Ember.Controller.extend({
    actions: {
      enter(){
        this.transitionToRoute('foo2');
      }
    }
});
```

This controller has one action called `enter` that transitions to the route called `foo2`. The `this.transitionToRoute` method is used to transition to different routes in the application. It takes two arguments. The first argument is the name of the route. The second argument is optional, and it is where you enter in the model. By default, it will be serialized in the URL if added.

The `trasintionToRoute` method can take route paths as well. For example, you might have a `foo2` nested route called `foo3`. You can transition to this route by calling `this.trasitionToRoute('foo2.foo3')`.

3. Add an action to the foo2 controller:

```
// app/controllers/foo2.js
import Ember from 'ember';

export default Ember.Controller.extend({
    actions: {
      enter(){
        this.transitionToRoute('foo1');
      }
    }
});
```

When the `enter` action is triggered, it transitions to the `foo1` route.

4. Update the foo1 template:

```
// app/templates/foo1.hbs
This is Foo1<br>

<button {{action 'enter'}}>Move to route foo2</button>
```

This `button` triggers the `enter action` in the `foo1` controller.

5. Update the foo2 template:

```
// app/templates/foo2.hbs
This is Foo2<br>
<button {{action 'enter'}}>Move to route foo1</button>
```

This button triggers the enter action in the foo2 controller.

6. Add a link to both the routes in the index template file:

```
// app/templates/index.hbs
{{link-to 'Foo1 Route' 'foo1'}}<br>
{{link-to 'Foo2 Route' 'foo2'}}<br>
```

This uses the link-to helper in a non-block form. The first argument is the name displayed and the second is the name of the route.

7. Update the application template file:

```
// app/templates/application.hbs
{{#link-to 'application'}}<h2 id="title">Welcome to
  Ember</h2>{{/link-to}}

{{outlet}}
```

The application template file has a link back to the application at the top.

8. Run ember server and you'll see the following screen after opening a web browser:

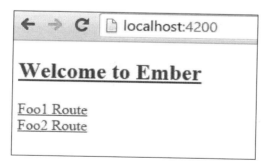

This displays a link to each route.

9. Click on the **Foo1 Route** link. The following page will be displayed:

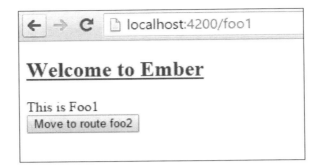

This displays the foo1 route.

10. Click on the **Foo2 Route** button. The following screen will be displayed:

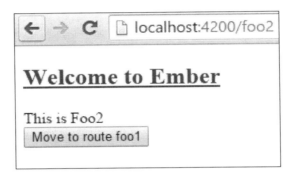

After the button is clicked, the foo2 route is displayed.

How it works...

To navigate through an application, we can use transitions inside a controller. The `trasitionToRoute` method is used to transition from one route to another. It's a part of the `Ember.Controller` class.

Managing dependencies between controllers

Often, controllers will need to access other controllers' properties and models. This is especially important when you have nested resources. In this recipe, we'll take a look at a nested controller that needs access to the parent controller's model and properties.

How to do it...

1. In a new application, generate a couple of new routes and templates:

```
$ ember g route foo1
$ ember g route foo1/foo2
$ ember g controller foo1
$ ember g controller foo1/foo2
$ ember g template index
```

This generates the foo1 and foo2 routes and controllers. The foo2 route is a nested route. The index template will contain links.

2. Verify in the router.js file that all the routes have been created correctly:

```
// app/router.js
import Ember from 'ember';
import config from './config/environment';

const Router = Ember.Router.extend({
  location: config.locationType
});

Router.map(function() {
  this.route('foo1', function() {
    this.route('foo2');
  });
});

export default Router;
```

As we generated the routes, router.js should already be set up for us. As you can see, the foo2 route is nested under the foo1 route. What this means is that we'll have to access the URL at /foo1/foo2 to access the foo2 route.

3. Add a new model to the foo1 route:

```
// app/routes/foo1.js
import Ember from 'ember';

export default Ember.Route.extend({
    model() {
      return ['abc','def','ghi'];
    }
});
```

All this route does is return a model with a simple array of letters.

4. Add a new model to the foo2 route:

```
// app/routes/foo1/foo2.js
import Ember from 'ember';

export default Ember.Route.extend({
    model() {
      return ['jkl','mno','pqr'];
    }
});
```

The nested `foo2` route also returns a simple array of letters in its `model` hook.

5. Add a new property to the foo1 controller:

```
// app/controlers/foo1.js
import Ember from 'ember';

export default Ember.Controller.extend({
    prop1: 'foo property'
});
```

This controller has one string property.

6. Create a property in the foo2 controller that can access the `foo1` model and properties:

```
// app/controllers/foo1/foo2.js
import Ember from 'ember';

export default Ember.Controller.extend({
    foo1Controller:Ember.inject.controller('foo1'),
    foo1: Ember.computed.reads('foo1Controller.model')
});
```

`Ember.inject.controller` allows us access to the `foo1` controller and properties. We can then use the `Ember.computed.reads` method to set the `foo1` property. This creates a read-only computed property that we can use in the template.

7. Update the foo1 template file:

```
// app/templates/foo1.hbs
<h3>Foo1</h3>

{{#each model as |letters|}}
    {{letters}}<br>
{{/each}}
{{outlet}}
```

All the `foo1` template does is display the list from the model.

8. Update the foo2 template file:

```
// app/templates/foo1/foo2.hbs
<h3>Foo2</h3>

{{#each model as |letters|}}
    {{letters}}<br>
{{/each}}
<h3>Here is the model injected in from the foo1 controller</h3>
{{#each foo1 as |letters|}}
    {{letters}}<br>
{{/each}}

<h3>Foo1 property</h3>
{{foo1Controller.prop1}}
```

The `foo2` template has access to all the properties of the `foo2` and `foo1` controllers. In this example, we can use the `each` helper to list all the letters in the `foo2` model. It can also use the `foo1` computed property to list all the letters in the `foo1` controller. We can even access individual properties using `foo1Controller`.

9. Add some basic links to the application and index template files:

```
// app/application.hbs
{{#link-to 'application'}}
  <h2 id="title">Welcome to Ember</h2>{{/link-to}}

{{outlet}}
```

The application file will have a link at the top:

```
// app/templates/index.hbs
{{link-to 'Foo1 Route' 'foo1'}}<br>
{{link-to 'Foo2 Route' 'foo1.foo2'}}
```

The `link-to` helpers here link to the `foo1` and `foo2` routes.

10. Start the Ember server and you'll see the following screen after you open a web browser:

The index home screen displays a link to each route.

11. Click on **Foo2 Route**. The following window will be displayed:

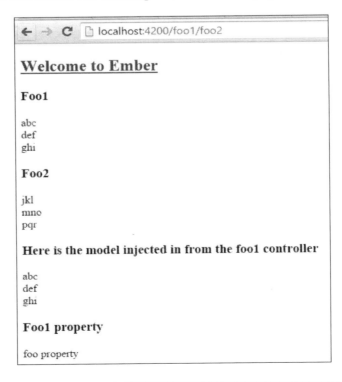

As you can see, the `foo1` template is displayed as well as the `foo2` template. The `foo2` template has access to both the `foo2` and `foo1` properties and model.

How it works...

Controllers can access other controllers using `Ember.inject.controller`. This is known as **dependency injection**. Dependency injection occurs when we take one object and inject it into another. Dependency injection is covered in more detail in the *Using dependency injection* recipe of *Chapter 11, Real-Time Web Applications*.

6

Ember Components

In this chapter, you'll learn the following recipes:

- ▶ Using components in an application
- ▶ Using events in components
- ▶ Implementing actions in components
- ▶ Passing properties to a component
- ▶ Using yield with components

Introduction

Components are a major feature of Ember.js. With components, you can encapsulate code and create widgets and custom tags. In addition, you can pass properties to a component, handle events and actions, and wrap content inside of it. Often, it can take the place of your controller.

Components align closely to the **W3C** custom elements specification. The W3C specification is still in consideration, although, given enough time, it will probably be adopted by the Web.

Using components in an application

Components can be used in applications in a variety of ways. In this recipe, we'll see how to create a component and add it to a template.

How to do it...

To begin, we'll create a simple component that displays student information.

1. In a new application, generate a new component:

   ```
   $ ember g component student-info
   ```

   All components must have a dash in their names. This will generate the `student-info` component. This stub will be created in the `app/components` and `app/templates/components` folders as well.

2. Edit the `student-info.js` file in the `app/components` folder. Add a few simple properties:

   ```js
   // app/components/student-info.js
   import Ember from 'ember';

   export default Ember.Component.extend({
       name: 'Erik',
       grade: 12,
       nickName: 'E'

   });
   ```

   In this component, we added three properties, `name`, `grade`, and `nickName`. We'll use these later in our template.

3. Update the component template in the `app/templates/components` folder:

   ```hbs
   // app/templates/components/student-info.hbs
   <br>student info:<br>
       {{name}}<br>
       {{grade}}<br>
       {{nickName}}<br>
   ```

   In this template, we are simply displaying information from the component.

4. Finally, let's edit the `application.hbs` file in the `app/templates` folder:

   ```hbs
   // app/templates/application.hbs
   <h2 id="title">Welcome to Ember</h2>
   {{student-info}}
   ```

The component is added to the application template by adding the Handlebars expression `{{student-info}}` to it. This will register an inline Handlebars helper automatically and render the contents of the `student-info.hbs` file to the `application.hbs` file.

Let's change this example and add the block form.

5. Edit the `student-info.hbs` file and add `yield` to it:

```
<br>student info:<br>
    {{name}}<br>
    {{grade}}<br>
    {{yield}}
    {{nickName}}<br>
```

The `{{yield}}` expression will be the placeholder where the outside template will render when the component is in block form. We'll discuss this more in the *Using yield with components* recipe.

6. Update the `application.hbs` file with the new block form component:

```
// app/templates/application.hbs
<h2 id="title">Welcome to Ember</h2>
{{#student-info}}
    This will render in the yield<br>
{{/student-info}}
```

The component has a hash (#) in front of the name. This is a signal to the Handlebars templating engine that the component will be in block form. The `yield` helper in the `student-info.hbs` file will display the contents in the block.

7. Run `ember server` and you'll see this output:

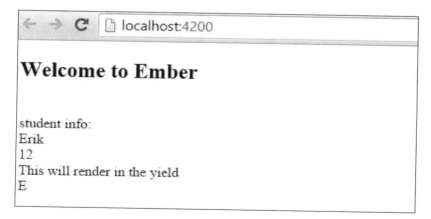

The students component is displayed here in the application template in block form.

All components are `div` tags. In other words, the component template that is created by default will be rendered in a `div` tag. This can be changed using the `tagName` property. You simply need to add this property to the component JavaScript file in the `components` directory.

Creating a student component dynamically

If needed, you can defer the selection of the component until runtime. Let's take a look at an example of doing this with the student component that we created in the earlier section.

1. In a new project, create a new `student-info` component:

    ```
    $ ember g component student-info
    ```

    This will generate the necessary files for the `student-info` component.

2. Edit the component file and add this information:

    ```
    // app/components/student-info.js
    import Ember from 'ember';

    export default Ember.Component.extend({
        name: 'Erik',
        grade: 12,
        nickName: 'E',

    });
    ```

    This component has a few simple properties.

3. Update the component template with this information:

    ```
    // app/templates/components/student-info.hbs
    <br>student info:<br>
        {{name}}<br>
        {{grade}}<br>
        {{yield}}
        {{nickName}}<br>
        {{moreInfo}}<br>
    ```

    Just as before, we are showing some simple properties that are retrieved from the component context.

4. Create a new application route in the `app/routes` folder. Add a new `model` method called `comp`:

```
// app/routes/application.js
import Ember from 'ember';

export default Ember.Route.extend({
    model() {
        return ['student-info'];

    }
});
```

This model sends back a string array. This array will be used in our template as the name of the component that we want to display dynamically.

5. Update the `application.hbs` file in the `app/templates` folder. Add a new `each` helper that will display the new dynamic component:

```
<h2 id="title">Welcome to Ember</h2>
{{#each model as |comp|}}
    {{component comp}}
{{/each}}
```

To display a dynamic component, you must use the `{{component}}` helper. The first argument of the helper is the name of the component that you want to use. In this case, `{{comp}}` is rendered to `student-info`. Note that we can use the component helper inline or in block form. If the component is rendered inline, `yield` is not used.

6. After running `ember server`, the template will render with the dynamic component:

Welcome to Ember

student info:
Erik
12
E

How it works...

Components are used to encapsulate data into a form that can be easily reused throughout an application. Each component can be in block or inline form and is rendered as a `div` tag by default. Components have a template and JavaScript file.

Using events in components

When creating components, you can attach events to them. Let's take a look at an example of this.

How to do it...

1. In a new project, generate a new component called `student-info`:

    ```
    $ ember g component student-info
    ```

    This will generate a component file in the `component` directory and the `templates/components` folder.

2. Edit the `app/components/student-info.js` file. Add a new `click` event:

    ```javascript
    // app/components/student-info.js
    import Ember from 'ember';

    const {$}= Ember
    export default Ember.Component.extend({
        click() {
            $('html').fadeToggle( 'slow', 'linear');
            $('html').delay(250).fadeIn();
        }
    });
    ```

    The first thing that you'll notice in this example is that we are using the ES2015 destructuring assignment. The destructuring assignment syntax extracts data from arrays or objects. Instead of typing `Ember.$` everywhere, I can just type `$`.

    Ember CLI by default has jQuery installed. We are using the jQuery syntax to fade the HTML document and fade it back after the component is clicked.

We aren't limited to just the `click` event though. There are several events that are available to Ember:

- ❑ Touch events:

  touchStart

  touchMove

  touchEnd

  touchCancel

- ❑ Keyboard events:

  keyDown

  keyUp

  keyPress

- ❑ Mouse events:

  mouseDown

  mouseUp

  contextMenu

  click

  doubleClick

  mouseMove

  focusIn

  focusOut

  mouseEnter

  mouseLeave

- ❑ Form events:

  submit

  change

  focusIn

  focusOut

  input

☐ HTML5 drag and drop events:

```
dragStart
drag
dragEnter
dragLeave
dragOver
dragEnd
drop
```

3. For the last step, we need to add the component to our application template. There is no need to edit the component template. For now, we'll just set the component to be in block form so that any click on the element will trigger the event:

```
// app/templates/application.hbs
<h2 id="title">Welcome to Ember</h2>

{{#student-info}}
    Student info block
{{/student-info}}
{{outlet}}
```

The `student-info` component is in block form. Click anywhere in the block to trigger the `click` event and cause the HTML document to fade.

There is an `index.html` file in the root of the `app` folder. This file has the default HTML and `head` tags. It also contains some links to your CSS and vendor files. You may notice that there are `{{content-for}}` helpers. These are used with Ember add-ons and should not be deleted.

4. Run `ember server` and the template should render as follows:

The HTML document will fade if any part of the student info block `div` is clicked.

How it works...

Ember events in components work by adding the name of the event as a method in the component. These events are fired in the template that the component has been added to. Components, by default, are `div` tags. So, any event that occurs must occur in the context of the `div` tag in the template that is rendered.

Ember supports several different types of events, including double-clicking, HTML 5 drag and drop events, and touch events. Custom events can be registered using the `Ember. Application.customEvents` method.

Implementing actions in components

Components can communicate changes with actions. These actions can be sent back to the parent or be handled in the component. Let's take a look at a few recipes that show this.

How to do it...

In this recipe, we'll create a student list that we will then manipulate.

1. In a new project, generate a `student-list` component:

    ```
    $ ember g component student-list
    ```

    This will generate the `student-list` component and the necessary files.

2. Update the `student-list.js` file in the `app/components` folder. We'll need to create a few `actions` and a new array:

    ```
    // app/components/student-list.js
    import Ember from 'ember';

    export default Ember.Component.extend({
        init() {
          this._super(...arguments);
          this.setup();
        },
        actions: {
          remove(){
            this.get('listOfStudents').popObject();
          },
          reset(){
            this.setup();
          }
    ```

```
  },
  setup(){
    let st = this.set('listOfStudents',[]);
    st.clear();
    st.pushObject('Erik');
    st.pushObject('Bob');
    st.pushObject('Suze');


  }

});
```

The first part of this component is the `init` method. This will fire as soon as the component is initialized. This is a private method that sets up the component. As we are overriding this framework method, we must call `super` so that the component is created correctly. The `setup` method is then called.

The `setup` method creates a new `listOfStudents` array, clears it, and creates three new string objects by popping them onto the array. As we are creating the `listOfStudents` array in the `init` method, it will be local to this component instance. It's good practice to declare objects or properties in the `init` or `didInsertElement` methods. Otherwise, if the object or array is declared as a property of the component, the component will no longer have its own independent state. We'll be discussing the `didInsertElement` hook later in the book.

There are two `actions` listed, `remove` and `reset`. Both will tie back into actions in the component's template that we'll use later. The `remove` action removes or pops off one object from the top of the array. The `reset` method calls `setup`, and this returns the component to its original state.

3. Add a couple of buttons and use the `each` helper to list the contents of the array in the `student-list.hbs` file in the `app/templates/components` folder:

```
// app/templates/components/student-list.hbs
<button {{action 'remove'}}>Remove</button>
<button {{action 'reset'}}>Reset</button><br>
{{#each listOfStudents as |student|}}
    {{student}}<br>
{{/each}}
```

The `{{action}}` helper will fire when the `remove` and `reset` buttons are pressed. The first argument to the `action` helper is always the action name. The `each` helper lists the contents of the `listOfStudents` Ember array.

4. For the last part, add the `student-list` component to the application template:

```
// app/templates/application.hbs
<h2 id="title">Welcome to Ember</h2>
{{student-list }}
{{outlet}}
```

This will display the contents of the `student-list` component.

5. After starting `ember server`, your output will look as follows:

Pressing the **Remove** button will remove each item one by one. The `Reset` button will reset the array back.

Closure actions with our student component

Ember provides you with a way to send actions from a parent to child component. We can use closure actions to make this possible.

1. In a new project, generate a new `application` route and a `student-list` component:

```
$ ember g route application
$ ember g controller application
$ ember g component student-list
```

This will generate the `application.js` file in the `app/routes` folder, the `application` controller, and the `student-list` component.

2. In the application route file, add a new `listOfStudents` array:

```
// app/routes/application.js
import Ember from 'ember';

export default Ember.Route.extend({
    listOfStudents: [],
    beforeModel(){
      this.reset();
    },
    model(){

      return this.get('listOfStudents');
    },
    reset(){
      let st = this.get('listOfStudents');
      st.clear();
      st.pushObject('Tiffany');
      st.pushObject('Zack');
      st.pushObject('George');
    },
    actions: {
      removeRoute(){
        this.get('listOfStudents').popObject();
      },
      resetRoute(){
        this.reset();
      }
    }
});
```

This might look familiar to you from the previous example. Here, we are creating a new array called `listOfStudents`. The `beforeModel` hook will run before the model is set up. In this `beforeModel`, the `reset` method is called. This adds the default data to the array.

The model hook returns the `listOfStudents` array. In addition, we added two actions, `remove` and `reset`, to remove an item or reset the items back to the original array, respectively.

This was essentially the same code that we had in the component earlier but we moved it to the route instead.

3. Edit the `application.hbs` file and add the component that we just created:

```
// app/templates/application.hbs
<h2 id="title">Welcome to Ember</h2>
{{student-list onRemove=(action 'removeController' )
onReset=(action 'resetController')}}
{{#each model as |student|}}
    {{student}}<br>
{{/each}}
{{outlet}}
```

This template will show a list of students from our model and our `student-list` component. The `onRemove` and `onReset` properties are set to actions that are basically functions in our parent controller that we can pass to the component. This is called a **closure action**. All closure actions must have parentheses surrounding the `(action 'removeController')` action.

4. Add two new actions to the controller:

```
// app/controllers/application.js
import Ember from 'ember';

export default Ember.Controller.extend({
    actions:{
      removeController(){
        this.send('removeRoute');
      },
      resetController(){
        this.send('resetRoute');
      }
    }
});
```

These two actions use `this.send` to send the action to the `removeRoute` and `resetRoute` actions that we defined earlier. You can use the `send` method to trigger actions from parent routes or controllers.

5. Update the component template file:

```
// app/templates/components/student-list.hbs
<button {{action 'removeComponent'}}>Remove</button>
<button {{action 'resetComponent'}}>Reset</button>
```

This component displays two buttons that are linked to actions that are defined in the component.

6. Update the component JavaScript file with the two new actions:

```
// app/components/student-list.js
import Ember from 'ember';

export default Ember.Component.extend({
    actions: {
      removeComponent(){
        this.get('onRemove')();
      },
      resetComponent(){
        his.attrs.onReset();
      }
    }
});
```

These actions will be triggered from the component template. At this point, they'll trigger the function that was passed to it from the closure actions, `onRemove` and `onReset`.

To invoke these methods, you can do it using either `this.get` or `this.attrs`. The `this.get` method and the name of the property, in this case `onRemove`, will invoke the method passed to it.

In the other case, you can use `this.attrs` to access the attributes on the property to invoke the function that was passed on, `this.attrs.onReset()`.

The action will flow this way: **application template -> component -> controller -> route**. The end result is the route triggering the action to remove or reset the list.

7. Run `ember server` and you should see a list that you can now delete or reset:

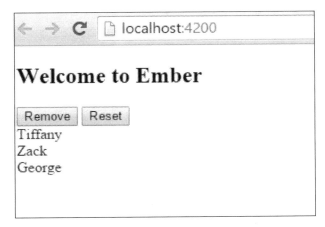

8. Clicking on the **Remove** or **Reset** buttons will trigger an action that was passed in from the controller. This action will bubble up to the route to reset or remove an item from the list.

How it works...

Actions can be handled in a few ways in a component. Actions can be added to different HTML tags and be handled within components. Actions can also be sent to parent components or controllers using closure actions or send.

Closure actions make the passing of actions much easier. We can pass down actions to components that they can then invoke. This helps separate logic between different parent routes, controllers, and components.

Passing properties to a component

Components by default are isolated from their surroundings. Any data that the component needs must be passed in. In this recipe, we'll create a student list. However, we will pass data to the component to be rendered.

How to do it...

1. In a new application, generate a new component and the `application` route:

   ```
   $ ember g route application
   $ ember g component student-list
   ```

   This will generate the `application.js` file in the `routes` folder and the files necessary from the `student-list` component.

2. Edit the `application.js` file in the `app/routes` folder:

   ```
   // app/routes/application.js
   import Ember from 'ember';

   export default Ember.Route.extend({
       model() {
         return ['Jim','Jeff','Jill']
       }
   });
   ```

   This model will return a simple array.

3. Update the `student-list` template in the `app/templates/components` folder:

    ```
    // app/templates/components/student-info.hbs

    {{#each compModel as |student|}}
        {{student}}<br>
    {{/each}}
    ```

    This will take the `compModel` property and iterate over it using the `each` helper.

4. Edit the `application.hbs` file in the `app/templates` folder. Add the new `student-info` component:

    ```
    // app/templates/application.hbs
    {{student-list compModel=model}}

    {{outlet}}
    ```

    The `student-list` template has the `compModel` property. This property passes in the model that is the application model that we set up earlier in the route. Keep in mind that `compModel` is accessed from the inside of the component. The model is accessed outside the component. The component does not have any access to the model unless it's passed to it.

5. Run `ember server` and you should see a list of elements in the model:

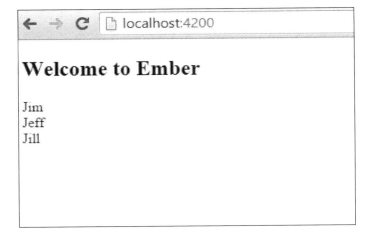

How it works...

Components are isolated sets of code that do not have access to the outside world. In other words, components must have any data that it needs passed to it. You can set this up by adding properties after the name of the component in the Handlebars expression.

Using yield with components

Components can be set up in block or inline form. When in block form, components can yield information. In this recipe, we'll look at an example of using yield to show information in a template.

How to do it...

1. In a new project, create a new student component:

    ```
    $ ember g component student-info
    ```

    This will create the student component.

2. Edit the `student-info` template file and add some text:

    ```
    // app/templates/components/student-info.hbs
    This is information before the yield<br>
    {{yield}}
    This is information after the yield
    ```

    The `{{yield}}` expression in the component will be where the text in the block will be rendered.

3. Add the new `student-info` component to the application template file:

    ```
    // app/templates/application.hbs
    <h2 id="title">Welcome to Ember</h2>

    {{#student-info}}
        Information in block<br>
    {{/student-info}}
    ```

    When in block form, designated by the hash #, the information in the block will show up in `{{yield}}`.

4. After running `ember server`, the following screen will be displayed:

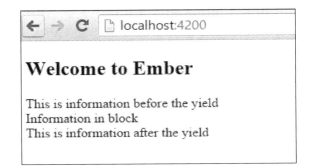

As you can see, the component `yield` template displayed the information in the block.

How it works...

The `{{yield}}` Handlebars expression works by taking the information in the component block and rendering it. The block form is designated by the hash, #. Inline components do not have the hash and do not yield information.

7
Ember Models and Ember Data

In this chapter, you'll learn the following recipes:

- ▶ Understanding the functionalities of Ember Data
- ▶ Creating, reading, updating, and deleting records with Ember Data
- ▶ Using fixtures
- ▶ Customizing the adapter and serializer
- ▶ Working with relationships

Introduction

Models are objects in Ember that represent data that can be displayed to users. They are persistent and won't be lost when the user closes the browser window.

Many models are loaded from data that is stored in a server from a database. Typically, the data is sent back and forth as a JSON representation. This is where Ember Data comes in. Ember Data is included by default when you create an application in Ember. It helps retrieve data, store data locally, and save information to the server.

Ember Data can be configured to work with many different types of databases and servers. If used properly, Ember Data can help manage your application models without the use of multiple Ajax requests throughout your application.

Understanding the functionalities of Ember Data

Ember Data uses a single data store that can be accessed throughout an application. In this example, we'll create a simple application that retrieves a list of books and displays it to the user.

Getting ready

Before we begin, we'll need to mock data for our server. Ember CLI has a built-in mock server that can handle this situation by generating a basic **Express server**. However, for the purposes of this recipe, we'll go ahead and use the Ember CLI Mirage add-on. It has more features and is easier to use. You can find more information about Ember CLI Mirage at `https://github.com/samselikoff/ember-cli-mirage`.

1. To begin, let's create a new application:

   ```
   $ ember new BookExample
   ```

2. After the application has been created, let's install the add-on:

   ```
   $ cd BookExample
   $ ember install ember-cli-mirage
   $ ember g factory book
   ```

   This will install the latest Bower and `npm` packages needed and create the `book` factory for Mirage.

   To make this recipe work, we'll need to mock book data.

3. Edit the `config.js` file in the `app/mirage` folder:

   ```
   // app/mirage/config.js
   export default function() {

       this.get('/books');
       this.get('/books/:id');
   }
   ```

   This configuration file will set the fake routes that we need for our data. The `/books` route will return all the book data and the `/books/:id` route will return individual books based on the ID passed in the URL.

4. Update the `book.js` file in the `app/mirage/factories` folder. Add the following properties:

```
// app/mirage/factories/book.js
import Mirage, {faker}  from 'ember-cli-mirage';

export default Mirage.Factory.extend({

    title: faker.lorem.sentence,   // using faker
    author() {return faker.name.findName(); },
    year: faker.date.past
});
```

This file sets the properties that we'll use later for our model. The `title` property refers to the name of the book, `author` refers to the person who wrote the book, and `year` is the year it was published. To make things a little easier, Ember CLI Mirage includes a library called `faker`. This library generates data that we can use to populate our in-memory data store.

5. Update the `default.js` file in the `app/mirage/scenarios` folder:

```
export default function( server ) {

    server.createList('book',10);
}
```

Make sure to delete the comments around `server`. This scenario will generate ten new `'book'` records every time the browser is loaded. After the browser is loaded, the books will be generated via the factory.

How to do it...

1. Begin by creating a model file for our books, a REST adapter, and a route:

```
$ ember g model book title:string author:string year:date
$ ember g adapter application
$ ember g route books
$ ember g route application
```

This command will generate a new model called `book`, and set the `title`, `author`, and `year` as properties in this model. The generate `adapter` command will create a new adapter for our application, while the last commands will generate routes for the `book` and `application`.

2. Open the `book.js` file in the `app/models` folder. It should look as follows:

```
// app/models/book.js
import DS from 'ember-data';

export default DS.Model.extend({
    title: DS.attr('string'),
    author: DS.attr('string'),
    year: DS.attr('date')
});
```

The `models` file is a representation of the data that we'll be using. We can use three different types of data: `string`, `number`, or `date`. This data will be loaded from our mock server.

3. Open the `application.js` file created in the `app/adapters` folder:

```
// app/adapters/application.js
import DS from 'ember-data';

export default DS.RESTAdapter.extend({
});
```

Ember Data has several adapters available for it. One of the easiest to use is the REST adapter.

4. The REST adapter data expects the data from the server in this format:

```
{
  "books": [
    {
      "id": 1,
      "title": "Some title",
      "author": "Authors name",
      "date": "1980-05-23"
    }
    {
      "id": 2,
      "title": "Some other title",
      "author": "Authors name 2",
      "date": "1985-05-23"

    }
  ]
}
```

The preceding JSON lists an array of books. If, by chance, only one record was returned, the REST adapter would expect the array to be named `book` and not `books`. Keep in mind that you should camel-case all record names and the data should be in the REST adapter format.

5. We'll need to be able to retrieve data from our data store and present it to the user. Edit the `application.js` file in the `app/routes` folder. Add a new model that returns all the books listed:

```
// app/routes/application.js
import Ember from 'ember';

export default Ember.Route.extend({
    model() {
        return this.store.findAll('book');
    }
});
```

As discussed in *Chapter 4, Ember Router*, one of the responsibilities of the route is returning the model data. The Ember Data store has a method called `findAll` that will return all the data from the `book` model. By convention, the Ember application will execute an HTTP GET to the `/book/` URL and expect a JSON payload in response. As this model is in the application route, it can be accessed in any template.

6. Update the `application.hbs` file and display the new data from the mock server:

```
// app/templates/application.hbs
{{#link-to 'index'}}<h2 id="title">Welcome to
    Ember</h2>{{/link-to}}

{{outlet}}

{{#each model as |book|}}
    <br>
    title: {{#link-to 'books'
      book.id}}{{book.title}}{{/link-to}}<br>
{{/each}}
```

This template uses the `each` helper to iterate though all the data that is returned from the `model` hook after the page loads. The `link-to` helper will pass `book.id` in the URL as an argument. We'll use the book `title` as the link.

7. Update the books route so that it returns a single record:

```
// app/routes/books.js
import Ember from 'ember';

export default Ember.Route.extend({
    model(params) {
        return this.store.findRecord('book', params.book_id);
    }
});
```

The `model` hook receives a parameter from the URL. The `findRecord` Ember Data can be used to find individual records. It will make an HTTP GET request to the `/books/:id` URL when the `model` hook is loaded. The first argument is the data store and the second is the record ID.

8. Update the `router.js` file in the `app` folder with the new dynamic route for `books`:

```
// app/router.js
import Ember from 'ember';
import config from './config/environment';

var Router = Ember.Router.extend({
    location: config.locationType
});

Router.map(function() {
    this.route('books', {path:'/books/:book_id'});
});

export default Router;
```

This new route for `books` has a path of `/books/:book_id`. To access the `books` route, you have to submit an ID in the path.

9. Update the `books.hbs` template:

```
// app/templates/books.hbs
{{outlet}}
<br>
<b>Author: {{model.author}}</b><br>
<b>Year: {{model.year}}</b>
<br>
```

Accessing this route will trigger the `model` hook. This will render `author` and `year` of the book selected.

10. Run `ember server` and open a web browser. You'll see a list of all the titles with links to each individual book:

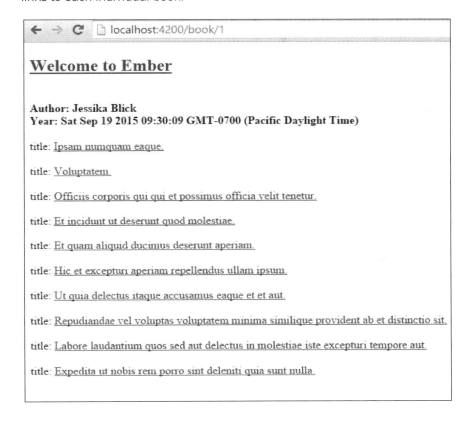

Each post has a unique ID. Clicking on a link will display the title and author of that book.

How it works...

Models represent data in Ember. These models can use Ember Data to store, update, and retrieve data from a server. The data from the server is usually sent in the JSON format. Ember offers a handful of adapters to the interface with the data coming from the server. The REST adapter is the most commonly used. It expects data in a certain format so that Ember can parse, store, and display it to the user.

Ember Data caches the data after it retrieves the data from the server. This minimizes the amount of round-trips to the server. However, Ember Data will make a request in the background whenever a cached data record is returned from the store. If the data has changed, it will be rerendered on the screen.

Creating, reading, updating, and deleting records with Ember Data

In the previous recipe, we retrieved already existing book data from our mock server and displayed it to the user. Ember Data also has the ability to create, delete, and even update records from the data store. We will be looking at these methods and more.

Getting ready

Just like the previous example, we'll need to install Ember CLI Mirage. Take a look at the previous recipe for instructions on this process. We'll be using the same factories as the book recipe and we'll be adding new methods to add, edit, and delete data.

1. In the `mirage` folder, open the `config.js` file:

```
// app/mirage/config.js
export default function() {

    this.get('/books');
    this.get('/books/:id');
    this.put('/books/:id');
    this.post('/books');
    this.delete('/books/:id');
}
```

   This will mock our backend and allow us to create, update, and delete data. This is done using the HTTP PUT, POST, and DELETE requests. We'll use this later in our program.

2. Update the `book.js` file in the `app/mirage` folder:

```
// app/mirage/factories/book.js
import Mirage, {faker}  from 'ember-cli-mirage';

export default Mirage.Factory.extend({

    title: faker.lorem.sentence,   // using faker
    author() {return faker.name.findName(); },
    year: faker.date.past
});
```

   This factory will be used to generate fake data that the Mirage in-memory database will return.

3. Update the `default.js` file in the `scenarios` folder:

```
// app/mirage/scenarios/default.js
export default function( server ) {

    server.createList('book',10);
}
```

Every time that the application loads, the server will create `10` `book` objects.

How to do it...

For this recipe, we'll be adding to the book example that we had in the *Understanding the functionalities of Ember Data* recipe.

1. Create a route called `new` and controller named `books`:

```
$ ember g route new
$ ember g controller books
$ ember g controller new
$ ember g controller application
```

This will generate the `new` route and `books` controller files.

2. Create a new template for the new route:

```
// app/templates/new.hbs
{{outlet}}
<b>title: {{input value=info.title size='15'}}</b><br>
<b>Author: {{input value=info.author size='15'}}</b><br>
<b>Year: {{input value=info.year size='35'}}</b><br>
<button {{action 'newText' }}>Submit Changes</button>
<button {{action 'cancel' }}>Cancel</button><br>
```

The new route will be used to add a new book to the repository. In this template, the `input` helper is used to create three textboxes. Each will be bound to the info property. A button at the bottom will submit the changes to the `newText` `action` method. The `cancel` button will trigger the `cancel` action.

3. Update the `new.js` controller with the new `actions` for `cancel` and `newText`:

```
// app/controllers/new.js
import Ember from 'ember';

export default Ember.Controller.extend({
    info: {},
```

```
actions:{
  newText(){
    let inf = this.get('info');
    let newBook = this.store.createRecord('book',{
      title: inf.title,
      author: inf.author,
      year: new Date(inf.year)
    });

    newBook.save().then((()=>{
      this.transitionToRoute('application');
      this.set('info',{});
    },()=> {
      console.log('failed');
    });
    },
    cancel(){
      return true;
    }


  }
});
```

4. There is a lot going on here; let's take a look at the `newText` action first:

```
newText(){
  let inf = this.get('info');
  let newBook = this.store.createRecord('book',{
    title: inf.title,
    author: inf.author,
    year: new Date(inf.year)
  });
```

In this action, we are getting the `info` property that was declared earlier. This property is an object that is used to store values from the template. The store has a method called `createRecord` that takes two arguments. The first argument is the model. The second is the object that we want to store. In this case, we want to add a new `book` record to the store. We use the `inf` object to set the `title`, `author`, and `year`.

5. Using the `createRecord` method doesn't persist the changes. The `save()` method is used to persist data back to the server:

```
newBook.save().then(()=>{
  this.transitionToRoute('application');
  this.set('info',{});
},()=> {
  console.log('failed');
});
```

The `save` method is a promise. It will either succeed or fail. If it succeeds, we use the `transitionToRoute` method to change the route back to the main application.

Afterwards, we set the `info` property back to an empty object. We do this so that the template `input` helper is cleared of all data. If it doesn't succeed, then we output an error to the console:

```
cancel(){
  return true;
}
```

The `cancel` action returns `true`. What this means is that instead of the controller handling it, it will be bubbled up to be handled by the route:

REST with Ember

When using the REST adapter in Ember, the `save()` method will send a PUT, DELETE, GET, or POST HTTP request to the server. The PUT request will be sent during an update. The DELETE request is used to delete a record. POST is used to add a new record, and the GET request is used to retrieve records. This is done by convention by the Ember REST adapter.

6. Update the `books.hbs` template file with a new action to update:

```
// app/templates/books.hbs
{{outlet}}
<br>
<b>title: {{input value=model.title size='15'}}</b><br>
<b>Author: {{input value=model.author size='15'}}</b><br>
<b>Year: {{input value=model.year size='35'}}</b><br>
<button {{action 'updateText'}}>Submit Changes</button>
<button {{action 'cancel'}}>cancel</button>
<br>
```

We've updated the books template to behave differently from our last example. In this example, it will allow us to edit the entries as follows:

title: Nulla voluptatem error i

Author: Kaleb Halvorson

Year: Thu Apr 02 2015 08:28:02 GMT-0700 (Pacific D

Submit Changes | cancel

7. Update the `books.js` controller to handle the new `updateText` and `cancel` actions:

```
// app/controllers/books.js
import Ember from 'ember';

export default Ember.Controller.extend({
    actions: {
      updateText(){
        let book = this.get('model');
        book.set('year',new Date(book.get('year')));
        book.save();
        this.transitionToRoute('application');
      },
      cancel() {
        return true;
      }
    }
});
```

The `updateText` action gets the current book `model`, sets the `year`, and then saves it. Afterwards, it transitions to the `application` route. If needed, we could handle the error condition if the save promise fails. For the sake of simplicity, we'll leave it as is. The `cancel` action returns `true`, which means that it will bubble up to the books route to be handled.

8. Update the `books.js` file in the route:

```
// app/routes/books.js
import Ember from 'ember';

export default Ember.Route.extend({
    model(params){
```

```
      return this.store.findRecord('book',params.book_id);
    },
    actions:{
      cancel() {
        return true;
      }
    }
});
```

The route file is the same as the previous recipe, except now we have a `cancel` action. This `cancel` action will be triggered after the controller returns `true`. By returning `true` here, the action bubbles up one more time to the application route.

9. Update the `new.js` route file:

```
// app/routes/new.js
import Ember from 'ember';

export default Ember.Route.extend({
    actions: {
      cancel() {
        return true;
      }
    }
});
```

This file will receive the action from the new controller. It also returns `true`, which means that the `cancel` action will be handled by the application route as well.

10. Update the application route file:

```
// app/routes/application.js
import Ember from 'ember';

export default Ember.Route.extend({
    model(){
      return this.store.findAll('book');
    },
    actions: {
      cancel(){
        this.transitionTo('application');
      }
    }
});
```

The cancel action in the application route handles the new and book routes cancel action. In either case, it will transition to the application route. In summary, the bubbling of the action went from the new controller to the new route and finally to the application route. If the cancel action was not included in the controller, by convention, the action will automatically bubble up.

11. We need to update the application template and add a new option to delete records. Update the application.hbs file with the new delete action:

```
// app/templates/application.hbs
{{#link-to 'index'}}<h2 id="title">Welcome to
  Ember</h2>{{/link-to}}
{{#link-to 'new'}}<h5>Add New Book</h5>{{/link-to}}

{{outlet}}

{{#each model as |book|}}
    <br>
    title: {{#link-to 'books'
      book.id}}{{book.title}}{{/link-to}} <br>
<a href="" {{action 'delete' book}}>delete?</a><br>
{{/each}}
```

The application will display each book. There is also a delete action button at the bottom of each record that passes in the book record.

12. Update the application controller to handle the new delete action:

```
// app/controllers/application.js
import Ember from 'ember';

export default Ember.Controller.extend({
    actions:{
      delete(book){
        book.deleteRecord();
        console.log(book.get('isDeleted'));
        book.save();
      }
    }
});
```

The book record has a method called deleteRecord. This deletes the record; however, it doesn't send the HTTP delete request to the server until save() is done. Another method called destroyRecord will delete and save at the same time. For this example, we'll use deleteRecord instead.

13. Load the Ember server and you'll see a list of records. You can click on each record and delete or edit it:

Welcome to Ember

Add New Book

title: [_____]
Author: [_____]
Year: [_____]
[Submit Changes] [Cancel]

title: Porro quidem eos voluptate nesciunt.
delete?

title: Illo veniam.
delete?

title: Alias quia fuga non deleniti.
delete?

title: Eaque ut et rem libero.
delete?

title: Sit ipsa incidunt voluptatem.
delete?

title: Eum cupiditate error a quia sint itaque libero dolorem.
delete?

title: Similique omnis officia cupiditate sed rem ipsam voluptatem eligendi officiis ad at error.
delete?

title: Similique suscipit sunt ad adipisci velit nam amet consectetur.
delete?

title: Sed fugiat et sapiente necessitatibus accusantium repellendus autem dolor in occaecati.
delete?

title: Soluta est officia eos quis ab eius eaque eum placeat enim.
delete?

Not using Ember Data?

Ember Data is the preferred method when working with a backend data store. However, it doesn't have to be the only option. When defining model information in a route, you can use Ajax methods or define your own repositories as well. You can use services and inject them throughout your application if needed. This will take a substantial amount of extra work, depending on your setup, but it is an option.

How it works...

Ember Data comes with several adapters that can be used to retrieve data from a backend server. The REST adapter allows the user to make requests to a backend server using HTTP GET, DETETE, PUT, and POST requests. By default, it expects responses in JSON.

The Ember Data store methods allow a user to find, delete, and save records. The Ember `save()` method triggers a response to the server. Before the save is done, records can be rolled back if needed.

Using fixtures

Fixtures are another way of mocking data. It's static data that can be used in our model to display to the user when testing our application. In this recipe, we'll see some basics on how to set it up with Ember CLI Mirage.

Getting ready

As with many of our other examples, we'll be using Ember CLI Mirage. Instead of using a factory, we'll set up fixture data.

1. Begin by creating a new application. Then add the Ember CLI Mirage add-on and generate the model and routes for the application:

   ```
   $ ember install ember-cli-mirage
   $ ember g model student name:string age:number
   $ ember g route index
   $ ember g adapter application
   $ ember g fixture students
   ```

   These commands will generate the basic structure of our app. In this application, fixture data will be used to display student information. For the sake of simplicity, we'll only be displaying this information and not manipulating it.

2. In the `mirage fixtures` folder, update the `students.js` file and add the fixture data:

```
// app/mirage/fixtures/students.js
export default [
    {id: 1, name: 'John', age: 17},
    {id: 2, name: 'Jack', age: 18},
    {id: 3, name: 'Suze', age: 17},
    {id: 4, name: 'Jane', age: 18}
];
```

The fixture data has four records. Each record has a different student's `name` and `age`. To use fixture data with Ember CLI Mirage, you must enter it as an array of objects.

3. Update the `config.js` file in the `mirage` folder. This file is used to set the `students` route:

```
// app/mirage/config.js
export default function() {

    this.get('/students');

}
```

This will set up a mock server endpoint for Ember Data to reach. By convention, Ember Data will look for the URL path of the pluralized model name. In this example, our model will be student; therefore, when Ember Data looks for data, it will do a GET request to `/students` on the server.

4. Add a new scenario to the `default.js` file for the fixture data:

```
// app/mirage/scenarios/default.js
export default function(server ) {
    server.loadFixtures();

}
```

The `loadFixtures()` command will load the fixtures in memory so that they are available to the `students` route.

How to do it...

1. Earlier, we created the model file. Let's take a look at it first to make sure that everything is set up correctly:

```
// app/models/student.js
import DS from 'ember-data';

export default DS.Model.extend({
    name: DS.attr('string'),
    age: DS.attr('number')
});
```

The `student` model has two properties called `name` and `age`.

2. Update the route `index.js` file to return the students model:

```
// app/routes/index.js
import Ember from 'ember';

export default Ember.Route.extend({
    model(){
        return this.store.findAll('student');
    }
});
```

The route file will return all `student` records using the `findAll` method. This will trigger an HTTP GET request to the server at `/students`. The `model` hook is triggered when you visit the route. By convention, Ember will then cache these results.

3. Open the application adapter. Set it to the REST adapter:

```
// app/adapters/application.js
import DS from 'ember-data';

export default DS.RESTAdapter.extend({
});
```

`RESTAdapter` will be used for all routes. It's a type of adapter that assumes that JSON data will be sent via XHR.

4. Edit the `index.hbs` file. This will display the model information:

```
// app/templates/index.hbs
{{#each model as |student|}}
    Name: {{student.name}}<br>
    age: {{student.age}}<br>
{{/each}}<br>
```

In this example, we use the `each` helper to iterate through all the records.

5. Run `ember server` and the following results should be displayed:

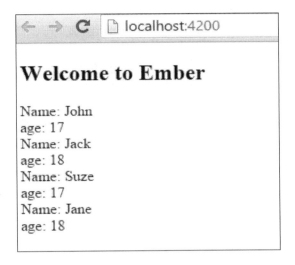

After the page loads, a list of the students' names and ages will be displayed. This data is retrieved from the fixture data that we set up earlier using our mock server.

How it works...

Fixtures are used when testing an application. It is well-known data and can be used for repeated tests. Ember CLI Mirage can be set up to use fixture data.

We'll be going over using fixture data with testing in the testing chapter in more detail.

Customizing the adapter and serializer

Ember Data is very opinionated on how it wants to access data. The adapter has built-in assumptions on what the data looks like. We can use serializers and adapters to change these assumptions.

For this recipe, we'll be building on the student application that we created in the previous section.

Getting ready

We'll be using the same application from the previous recipe. We'll need to edit Ember CLI Mirage to handle a new namespace.

In the `config.js` file in the `mirage` folder, update the `students` route:

```
// app/mirage/config.js
export default function() {

    this.get('api/v1/students');
}
```

This will change the endpoint to `api/v1/students` instead of just `/students`.

How to do it...

1. In the students application from the previous section, edit the `application.js` file in the `adapters` folder.

2. Add a new `namespace`:

   ```
   // app/adapters/application.js
   import DS from 'ember-data';

   export default DS.RESTAdapter.extend({
       namespace: 'api/v1'
   });
   ```

   The `namespace` property is used to prefix requests with a specific URL. In this case, all requests will have `api/v1` prepended to them.

3. Start the Ember server and you should see requests going to `/api/v1/students`.

Optional customizations in Ember Data

Ember offers a number of other customizations if needed. Here are a few important ones to keep in mind.

Host customization

In the adapter file, you can add a new location where Ember Data should send requests. This overwrites the default location of the local server:

```
// app/adapters/application.js
import DS from 'ember-data';

export default DS.RESTAdapter.extend({
host: 'https://api.example.com'
});
```

As an example, now all the requests will be sent to `api.example.com`.

Headers customization

Depending on the API, you may need to send specific headers in each HTTP request. You can add this using the `headers` property:

```
// app/adapters/application.js
import DS from 'ember-data';

export default DS.RESTAdapter.extend({
  headers: {
    'API_INFO:': 'key',
    'SECOND_HEADER': 'Some value'
  }
});
```

This will add new `headers` for every request that is sent. If needed, you can also use dynamic information in your headers by creating a computed property.

Working with serializers

When using Ember Data, serializers format the data that's sent and received from the backend data store. We can customize this data to fit the needs of our backend.

Updating IDs

By default, Ember Data expects each record to have an ID. We can change the name of this using the primary key property.

1. Generate a new `serializer` file:

    ```
    $ ember g serializer application
    ```

    This generates the `serializer` file that we can update.

2. Update the `application.js` serializer with the new ID:

    ```
    // app/serializers/application.js
    import DS from 'ember-data';

    export default DS.RESTSerializer.extend({
        primaryKey: '_id'
    });
    ```

    This will transform the ID property to `_id` when serializing and deserializing data. In other words, when data is sent or received from the server, it will have a primary key that is set to `_id`.

KeyForAttribute when working a JSON payload

At times, the data sent back from the server may not be in the correct format. For example, `RESTAdapter` expects the JSON payload attribute names in camel-case. We can change this using the `keyForAttribute` property:

```
// app/serializers/application.js
import DS from 'ember-data';

export default DS.RESTSerializer.extend({
    keyForAttribute(attr) {
      return Ember.String.decamelize(attr);
    }
});
```

For example, let's say that the data sent back from the server is underscored instead of camel-cased. The server is returning `school_name` instead of `schoolName`. This can be fixed using `keyForAttribute` and `decamelize`. This will take the model name `schoolName` and `decamelize` it to `school_name` so that it matches what's returned from the server.

How it works...

Adapters are used in Ember Data to help interpret data that is sent and retrieved from the server. It has a set of built-in assumptions on how the data should look. We can make changes so that we can accommodate different types of APIs. For example, we can customize the endpoint's path namespace as well as the host if needed.

Serializers format the data that is sent and received from the server. Ember Data expects data to be in a certain format. We can change many things in this data including the primary key and the keys in the JSON payload. This is accomplished by adding new properties to the serializer.

Working with relationships

When working with a data store, you'll need to be able to handle relationships. In this recipe, we'll go over some common relationships from one-to-many and many-to-one and also how to use it with Ember Data.

Getting ready

As with the other recipes, we'll be using Ember CLI Mirage to mock our backend. In this recipe, we'll create a simple one-to-many and many-to-one relationship. We'll mock a school that has instructors and classes. For every class, there is one instructor. Every instructor will have one or more classes.

1. Create a new Ember application. In this application, generate the following files:

   ```
   $ ember install ember-cli-mirage
   $ ember g model instructor
   $ ember g model class
   $ ember g route index
   $ ember g helper addone
   $ ember g adapter application
   $ ember g fixture classes
   $ ember g fixture instructors
   ```

   This will create the models, route, adapter, and helper that we'll need for this application.

2. In the `mirage fixtures` folder, update these two files, `classes.js` and `instructors.js`:

```
// app/mirage/fixtures/classes.js
export default [
    {id: 1, subject: 'History',instructor:[1]},
    {id: 2, subject: 'Spanish',instructor:[1]},
    {id: 3, subject: 'Government',instructor:[3]},
    {id: 4, subject: 'English',instructor:[2]},
    {id: 5, subject: 'German',instructor:[2]},
    {id: 6, subject: 'Social Studies',instructor:[4]},
    {id: 7, subject: 'Math',instructor:[]}
];
```

The `classes.js` file has a list of classes and subjects.

3. Create the `instructors.js` file:

```
// app/mirage/fixtures/instructors.js
export default [
    {id: 1, name: 'John', age: 17, classes:[1,2]},
    {id: 2, name: 'Jack', age: 18, classes:[4,5]},
    {id: 3, name: 'Suze', age: 17, classes:[3]},
    {id: 4, name: 'Jane', age: 16, classes:[6]}
];
```

As you can see, each young instructor has a list of classes that they teach. Each class has one, and only one, instructor for that class.

4. Edit the `config.js` file for Mirage. Add the new routes:

```
// app/mirage/config.js
export default function() {

    this.get('/instructors',['instructors','classes']);
    this.get('/classes',['instructors','classes']);
}
```

5. Each one of these endpoints will return the `instructor` and `class` data. This is done via **sideloading**. Here is an example of a JSON response sideloaded:

```
{
  "instructors": [
    {
      "id": 1,
      "name": "John",
      "age": "17",
      "classes": [1,2]
    },
```

```
    {
      "id": 2,
      "name": "Jack",
      "age": "18",
      "classes": [3,4]

    }
  ],
  "classes": [
    {
      "id": 1,
      "subject": "History",
      "instructor": [1]
    },
    {
      "id": 2,
      "subject": "Spanish",
      "instructor": [1]

    },
    {
      "id": 3,
      "subject": "Government",
      "instructor": [2]
    },
    {
      "id": 4,
      "subject": "English",
      "instructor": [2]

    },
  ]

}
```

As you can see from the preceding example, both the `instructor` and `class` data was returned. This is the default that `RESTAdapter` expects.

On the other hand, we could return the data using asynchronous relationships. When this occurs, the server data store returns records only for one model. Ember then does one or more HTTP requests to retrieve data for the other model. For the simplicity of this example, we'll assume that the data is sideloaded.

6. Finally, create a new scenario that loads the fixture data for us to use:

```
// app/mirage/scenarios/default.js
export default function( server ) {

    server.loadFixtures();
}
```

This will load both fixtures so that they can be returned to the Ember client.

How to do it...

1. Open the `application.js` file in the `adapter` folder. Set it to `RESTAdapter`:

```
import DS from 'ember-data';

export default DS.RESTAdapter.extend({
});
```

`RESTAdapter` will be used for this recipe.

2. Edit the `class.js` and `instructor.js` files in the `models` folder. Add the new properties for the model:

```
// app/models/class.js
import DS from 'ember-data';

export default DS.Model.extend({
  subject: DS.attr('string'),
  instructor: DS.belongsTo('instructor')
});
```

In this example, we need to make sure that the class has one `instructor`. This can be accomplished using the `DS.belongsTo` method. This tells Ember to look at the `instructor` model for this property.

3. The instructor has a one-to-many relationship with the class model. One instructor can have one or more classes that he teaches. We can accomplish this using the `DS.hasMany()` method and providing the name of the model:

```
// app/models/instructor.js
import DS from 'ember-data';

export default DS.Model.extend({
    name: DS.attr('string'),
    age: DS.attr('number'),
    classes: DS.hasMany('class')
});
```

4. Update the `index.js` file in the `routes` folder. Specify it to return all the `instructor` data:

```
// app/routes/index.js
import Ember from 'ember';

export default Ember.Route.extend({
    model() {
        return this.store.findAll('instructor');
    }
});
```

This route uses the Ember Data `findAll` method to return all the `instructor` data.

5. Update the `helper` file:

```
// app/helpers/addone.js
import Ember from 'ember';

export function addone(params) {
    return +params+1;
}


export default Ember.Helper.helper(addone);
```

Helpers in Ember are used to manipulate template data. You can pass information to one and return information. In this example, we are doing some simple mathematics.

6. Edit the `index.hbs` file with the model data:

```
// app/templates/index.hbs
{{outlet}}
{{#each model as |instructor|}}
Name of instructor: <b>{{instructor.name}}</b><br>
Teaches Classes:<br>
{{#each instructor.classes as |class index|}}
    <b>{{addone index}}: {{class.subject}}</b><br>
{{/each}}
<br>    <br>
{{/each}}
```

In this template, we are using the `each` helper to display the instructor's name. To access the class information, another `each` helper iterates over `instructor.classes`. In each iteration, we display the `subject` and index class. As the index starts at zero, we can pass it to the `addone` helper. This helper increments the number passed to it.

7. Run `ember server` and you should see all the data displayed from the fixture data:

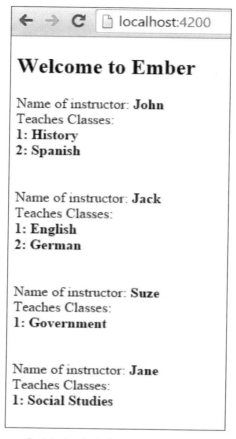

Each instructor is listed with each class

Ember uses the `DS.hasMany` and `DS.belongsTo` methods to signify a one-to-many and a one-to-one relationship. Ember, by convention, assumes that you are using the JSON API adapter. At the time of writing this, the JSON API is the default adapter for Ember Data. It communicates with a server via well-defined JSON via XHR. Its goal is to be easy to work with on the client and server side while working with a broad set of use cases, including relationships. For the most part, the REST adapter works fine. So, I've included it in the book instead of the JSON API adapter. Be aware that you can use either to accomplish your goals.

This can be changed using `RESTAdapter` instead. `RESTAdapter` assumes that all keys are camel-cased and that any data sent is sideloaded. This is done to help developers easily integrate their backend APIs and data stores with Ember.

8

Logging, Debugging, and Testing

In this chapter, we'll cover the following recipes:

- ► Using Ember.Logger
- ► Using Ember Inspector
- ► Verifying deprecations and using advanced features of Ember Inspector
- ► Using acceptance testing
- ► Using unit tests
- ► Testing components
- ► Testing routes
- ► Testing models
- ► Testing controllers

Introduction

Testing is an important part of the Ember framework. Ember allows three different classifications of tests—**acceptance**, **unit**, and **integration**.

Acceptance tests are used to test the application flow and interaction. It mimics the same actions that a user might have. For example, this could include filling out forms or navigating to different parts of an application.

Unit tests are used to test smaller chunks of functionality. This might include testing computed properties or checking fields for different element tags.

Integration tests are somewhere in between unit and acceptance tests. It's recommended to use them with component testing. For example, integration tests work well with testing UI and controls.

Creating test cases for your applications is a good practice, especially if this application will be used in production.

Using Ember.Logger

Ember.Logger is a robust type of logging in Ember. It goes beyond the capabilities of `imports.console`. In this recipe, we'll take a look at some examples on how to work with it in your application.

How to do it...

In this project, we'll create a simple program that demonstrates how to use some of the `Ember.logging` capabilities:

1. In a new program, add a new `index` route:

    ```
    $ ember g route index
    ```

    This will create a new `index` route.

2. Edit the `index.js` file in the `routes` folder. Add some new logging:

    ```
    // app/routes/index.js
    import Ember from 'ember';
    const {Logger}= Ember;
    export default Ember.Route.extend({
        model(){
           Logger.log('log');
           Logger.info('info', 'more stuff');
           Logger.error('error');
           Logger.debug('debug');
           Logger.warn('warn');
           Logger.assert(true === false);
           return {};
        }
    });
    ```

    `Ember.logging` gives us five different logging options. All these different types of `log` methods accept one or more arguments. Each argument will be joined together and separated by a space when written to the browser console window:

    ```
    Logger.log('log');
    ```

3. This is the basic form of logging in Ember. It simply logs the values to the browser console:

```
Logger.info('info', 'more stuff');
```

The `info` logger logs a message to the console as an `info` message. In Firefox and Chrome, a small **I** icon is displayed next to the item:

```
Logger.error('error');
```

The `error` log prints to the console with an **error** icon, red text, and stack trace.

```
Logger.debug('debug');
```

The `debug` log prints to the console in blue text.

```
Logger.warn('warn');
```

The warning log will print to the console with a **warning** icon.

```
Logger.assert(true === false);
```

The `assert` statement will return an error and stack trace if the value returns `false`.

4. Fire up the Ember server and open **Console**. This is a screenshot of how it looks in Chrome:

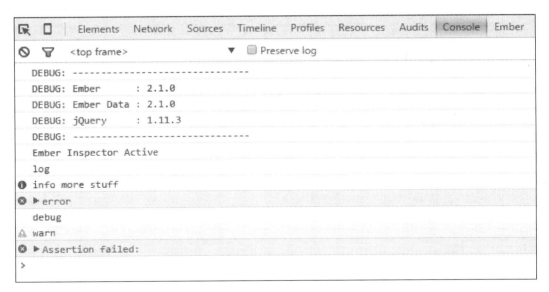

How it works...

The Ember.Logger is a more powerful console logger. It's a robust logging tool to make debugging easier. Ember.Logger is built-in in the Ember CLI package.

Using Ember Inspector

The Ember Inspector is an add-on for your browser that can help you debug your Ember app. In this recipe, we'll look at some examples on how to use it.

Getting ready

Before beginning, you must install the add-on. It's available for Chrome, Firefox, or Opera. Other browsers such as Internet Explorer can also be used via `bookmarklet`.

1. Install the browser add-on for Ember Inspector:

    ❑ For Firefox, install the add-ons from the following website: `https://addons.mozilla.org/en-US/firefox/addon/ember-inspector/`

    ❑ On Chrome, install the add-on from the Chrome web store: `https://chrome.google.com/webstore/detail/ember-inspector/bmdblncegkenkacieihfhpjfppoconhi`

    ❑ All other browsers visit the Ember Inspector Github page for further instructions: `https://github.com/emberjs/ember-inspector`

2. For the purposes of our recipe, we'll use Ember CLI Mirage to return a simple `school` model. After creating a new project, run this command:

    ```
    $ ember install ember-cli-mirage
    $ ember g factory school
    ```

    This will install all the necessary files so that we can mock an HTTP server.

3. After the add-on for Ember CLI Mirage is installed, update the `config.js` file in the `mirage` folder:

    ```
    // app/mirage/config.js
    export default function() {

        this.get('/schools');
    }
    ```

    This will add an HTTP GET route that our Ember client will connect when retrieving the school information.

4. Update the file for the school information in the `mirage/factories/` folder called `school.js`:

```
// app/mirage/factories/school.js
import Mirage, {faker}  from 'ember-cli-mirage';

export default Mirage.Factory.extend({

    name:faker.name.firstName,           // using faker
    city: faker.address.city,
});
```

This file will be used to generate fake names and city data for our fictitious school.

5. Update the `default.js` file:

```
// app/mirage/scenarios/default.js
export default function( server ) {

    server.createList('school', 2);
}
```

This will seed the data that we need from our factories for the application.

6. Generate an `index route`, `model`, and the REST `adapter`:

```
$ ember g route index
$ ember g model school name:string city:string
$ ember g adapter application
```

These files will be used in our application, which we'll discuss in the next section.

How to do it...

The purpose of this application is to return a list of schools. We'll be using the Ember Inspector to look at this data in more detail.

1. Open the `application.js` file in the `adapters` folder. Verify that the `RESTAdapter` is set:

```
// app/adapters/application.js
import DS from 'ember-data';

export default DS.RESTAdapter.extend({
});
```

This tells Ember to use the REST adapter with Ember Data. Review *Chapter 7, Ember Models and Ember Data,* on Ember Data for a refresher.

2. Edit the `school.js` file in the `models` folder:

```
// app/models/school.js
import DS from 'ember-data';

export default DS.Model.extend({
    name: DS.attr('string'),
    city: DS.attr('string')
});
```

This model has two properties, `name` and `city`.

3. Update the `index.hbs` file in the `app/templates` folder:

```
// app/templates/index.hbs
{{outlet}}

{{#each model as |schoolName|}}
    Name:{{schoolName.name}}<br>
    City:{{schoolName.city}}<br>
    <br>
{{/each}}
```

The `each` helper will iterate through every model returned and display the school information.

4. Update the `index.js` file in the `app/routes` folder:

```
// app/routes/index.js
import Ember from 'ember';

export default Ember.Route.extend({
    model() {
      return this.store.findAll('school');
    }
});
```

5. Run `ember server` and you'll see a list of schools, as illustrated in the following image:

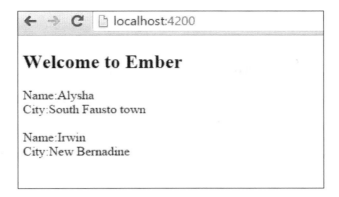

6. Let's open the Ember Inspector and see what it shows. In Chrome, you can access this by opening the console and clicking on the **Ember** tab:

The Ember Inspector shows **View Tree**, **Routes**, **Data**, **Deprecations**, and **Info**.

7. Click on **Info** in the Ember Inspector:

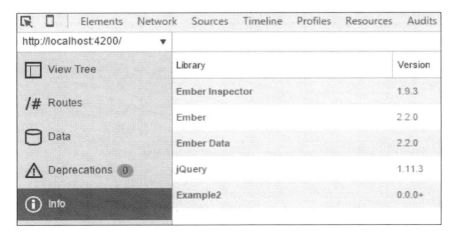

Info displays all the library information loaded in this application. This can be really useful in finding out what version everything is using.

8. Click on **View Tree** in the Ember Inspector:

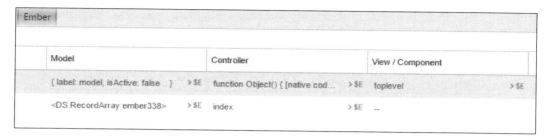

The **View Tree** shows all sorts of information about the application. It shows the current routes, templates, models, and more. This can be helpful to figure out what's currently loaded on the screen.

9. Click on **Routes** in the Ember Inspector:

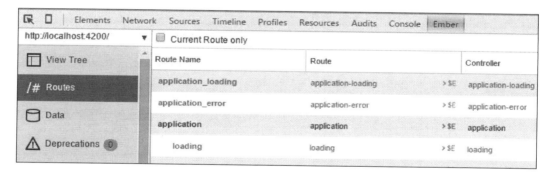

The **Routes** show all the available routes, controllers, and templates. Some routes may not be defined but will be displayed, such as **loading**.

10. Click on **$E** next to the **index** route:

Route Name	Route	
schools_loading	schools-loading	> $E
schools_error	schools-error	> $E
schools	schools	> $E
index_loading	index-loading	> $E
index_error	index-error	> $E
index	index	> $E

In the Inspector, you can assign instance variables by clicking on **$E**.

11. Open the console and add a new record using the instance variable, **$E**:

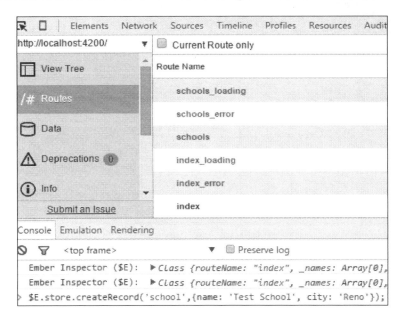

12. You can type the following in the console window in the browser:

```
$E.store.createRecord('school',{name: 'Test School', city:
'Reno'});
```

This will add a new record to your data store. The page will automatically update with this information. This is very valuable. You can use this anywhere to help troubleshoot issues.

13. Click on `Data` to see all the model data:

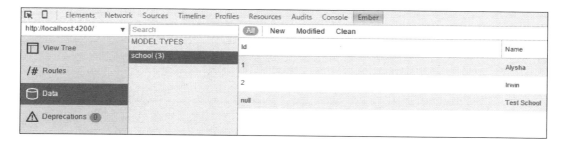

Optionally, you can click on any of this data and verify the attributes. You can make changes as well and it will automatically update to the screen.

Verifying deprecations and using advanced features of Ember Inspector

In this recipe, we will explore deprecations using advanced features of Ember Inspector.

How to do it...

Deprecation warnings will be displayed in deprecations. Check this to make sure that nothing in your application is deprecated. If deprecation is listed, it will have a link that you can click on to see what you need to do to fix it:

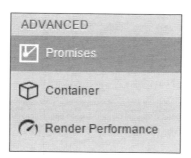

How it works...

Ember Inspector was designed to make the creating and debugging of Ember applications easier. It was created as an add-on for most modern web browsers. It displays your current application information, routes, templates, data, and more.

It's an open source add-on and has an active developer community behind it. New features are being added all the time. To request your own, check out the Github page here: `https://github.com/emberjs/ember-inspector`

Using acceptance testing

Acceptance tests generally help test workflows and emulate user interactions. In this recipe, we'll look at creating a few simple acceptance tests.

How to do it...

1. In a new application, create a new component called `book-shelf` and a new acceptance test called `add-book-test.js`:

   ```
   $ ember g component book-shelf
   $ ember g acceptance-test add-book
   ```

   This will create the code necessary for the `book-shelf` component and the `add-book` acceptance test. Keep in mind that an integration test will also be generated for the `book-shelf` component. We will not be updating the integration test in this example.

2. Update the component file with a new `books` array and new action:

   ```
   // app/components/book-shelf.js
   import Ember from 'ember';

   export default Ember.Component.extend({
       books: Ember.A([{name: 'Moby Dick'}]),
       actions: {
         add(val) {
           this.get('books').addObject({name:val});
         }
       }
   });
   ```

   This component uses the `books` property to keep track of books on the book shelf. The `books` property is an Ember array of objects. The `add` action adds another object to the array. `Ember.A` is used to declare an Ember array.

3. Update the `book-shelf.hbs` component template file:

```
// app/templates/components/book-shelf.hbs
{{input value=val}}
<button {{action 'add' val}}>Push Me</button><br>
<ul>
{{#each books as |book|}}
    <li>{{book.name}}<br></li>
{{/each}}
</ul>
```

The component lists all the books. It also has an `input` helper and `button`. The button has an action called `add` that gets triggered on the click event. It passes on the value from the `input` helper as an argument to `action`.

4. Add the `book-shelf` component to the application file:

```
<h2 id="title">Welcome to Ember</h2>
{{book-shelf}}
{{outlet}}
```

This code adds the `book-shelf` component to the application template.

5. Add the test code to the `add-book-test.js` file:

```
// app/tests/acceptance/add-book-test.js
import { test } from 'qunit';
import moduleForAcceptance from 'example3/tests/helpers/module-
for-acceptance';

moduleForAcceptance('Acceptance | add book');

test('visiting / and adding book', function(assert) {
    visit('/');
    fillIn('input','My new book');
    click('button');
    andThen(function() {
      assert.equal(currentURL(), '/');
      assert.equal(find('li:last').text(),'My new book');

    });

});
```

This acceptance test visits the root of the application at `/`. It then adds new text to the `input` helper and clicks the `button`. It then checks the URL and template to make sure the text was added.

The code at the top is mostly boilerplate. The tests are at the bottom and can be followed step by step. The `visit`, `fillIn`, `click`, and `andThen` helpers are all asynchronous test helpers.

The following is a list of all the asynchronous and synchronous test helpers:

- ▶ `click(selector)`: This clicks an element and triggers the corresponding action, and returns a promise that fulfils when asynchronous behavior is complete
- ▶ `fillIn(selector, value)`: This fills in the selected input with the values given, and returns a promise that fulfils when all asynchronous behavior is complete
- ▶ `keyEvent(selector, type, keyCode)`: This simulates keypress, keydown, or keyup on the element
- ▶ `triggerEvent(selector, type, options)`: This triggers the given event on the element identified by the `selector`
- ▶ `visit(url)`: This visits the route given by the URL, and returns a promise that is fulfilled when all asynchronous behavior is complete
- ▶ `currentPath()`: This returns the current path
- ▶ `currentRouteName()`: This returns the currently active route
- ▶ `currentURL()`: This returns the current URL
- ▶ `find(selector, context)`: This finds an element starting at the app's root element; optionally, you can add some context

6. Run `ember server` and visit the `/tests` URL. This URL will display all the tests running. Look for the acceptance test for add-book:

> 2. JSHint - acceptance: acceptance/add-book-test.js should pass jshint (1)
>
> 1. acceptance/add-book-test.js should pass jshint.

7. This acceptance test shows that everything passed. Alternatively, you can also run the tests on the command line:

```
$ ember test -server
```

8. This will bring up a screen so that you can run tests in your console. To use this, you must first navigate to `localhost` on port `7357`. This screen will then refresh with the number of passed tests:

```
TEST'EM 'SCRIPTS!
Open the URL below in a browser to connect.
http://localhost:7357/

    Chrome 46.0 |
    12/12 ✓     |
```

Each test will be checked, and any tests that fail will be shown on this screen. The test will be rerun after any file changes.

How it works...

Acceptance tests are used to test the user interaction and flow. This is done via Ember's QUnit testing framework, although other testing frameworks are supported using third-party add-ons. You can navigate to the `/tests` URL or run `ember test` on the server to execute test cases.

Using unit tests

Unit tests are used to test smaller chunks of functionality. In this recipe, we'll see an example of this.

How to do it...

In this example, we'll create a simple `Ember.Object` with a computed property. We'll test this computed property and assert if the value returned is correct or not.

1. In a new project, create a new `first-last.js` file in the `models` folder:

```
// app/models/first-last.js

import Ember from 'ember';

export default Ember.Object.extend({
    firstName: 'John',
```

```
      lastName: 'Smith',
      fullName: Ember.computed('firstName', 'lastName',
        function() {
        const firstName = this.get('firstName');
        const lastName= this.get('lastName');
        return `Full Name: ${firstName} ${lastName}`;
      })
});
```

In this file, we have two properties, `firstName` and `lastName`. The `fullName` computed property combines these two and returns a full name. If either of these properties change, the computed property will fire.

2. Create a new unit test that checks `Ember.Object` and `computed` property:

   $ ember g model-test first-last

   The `model-test` unit test generated will create a new test file in the `/tests/unit/models` directory.

3. Update the `first-last-test.js` file with a new unit test that checks to see whether the computed property is returning the correct values:

```
// tests/unit/models/first-last-test.js

import { moduleFor, test } from 'ember-qunit';

moduleFor('model:first-last', 'Unit | Model | fullName', {
    unit: true
});

test('check computed property fullName', function(assert) {
    const firstLast= this.subject();
    firstLast.set('firstName','Erik');
    firstLast.set('lastName','Hanchett');
    assert.equal(firstLast.get('fullName'),
      'Full Name: Erik Hanchett');
});
```

The `moduleFor` is a unit test helper provided by `ember-qunit`. This helps us get access to the model that we created for lookup and instantiation. The `unit: true` property flags the test case as a unit test. As we are using `moduleFor`, we can instantiate the `firstLast` object using `this.subject()`. The test then sets `firstName` and `lastName` of the computed properties and does `assert` to make sure that they are equal.

4. Run `ember server` and check the output of the `/tests` URL:

> 12. **Unit | Model | fullName: check computed property fullName (1)**
>
> 1. okay

The output shows that the unit tests passed

5. Update the `first-last-test.js` file with the wrong value:

```
// tests/unit/models/first-last-test.js
…
test('check computed property fullName', function(assert) {
    const firstLast= this.subject();
    firstLast.set('firstName','Erik');
    firstLast.set('lastName','Hanchett');
    assert.equal(firstLast.get('fullName'),
      'Full Name: Erik wrong');
});
```

We updated the code, so now the test will fail because the text does *NOT* match.

6. Navigate to the `/tests` folder and see the output:

> 12 Unit | Model | fullName: check computed property fullName (1, 0, 1) Rerun
>
> 1. failed
> Expected: "Full Name: Erik wrong"
>   Result: "Full Name: Erik Hanchett"
>   Diff: "Full Name: Erik wrongHanchett"
>   Source: at Object.<anonymous> (http://localhost:4200/assets/tests.js:167:12)
>   at Object.wrapper (http://localhost:4200/assets/test-support.js:2027:29)
>   at runTest (http://localhost:4200/assets/test-support.js:3949:28)
>   at Object.Test.run (http://localhost:4200/assets/test-support.js:3934:4)
>   at http://localhost:4200/assets/test-support.js:4076:11
>   at process (http://localhost:4200/assets/test-support.js:3737:24)

Now the test fails because the text does not match. You can see this output by navigating to the `/tests` folder or running `ember test` from the command line.

How it works...

Unit tests are used to test small pieces of code or functionality. They are another part of the Ember QUnit library. Unit tests can run for virtually anything in your application, including models, components, or controllers.

Testing components

Components should be tested using integration tests. In this recipe, we'll look at a simple example of a component that changes the size of the text.

How to do it...

1. In a new application, create a new component called `font-sizer`:

    ```
    $ ember g component font-sizer
    ```

    This will generate a new component called `font-sizer`. This component will be used to resize text.

2. Update the `font-sizer.js` file in the `components` folder:

    ```
    // app/components/font-sizer.js
    import Ember from 'ember';

    export default Ember.Component.extend({
        textInfo: 'Hello World',
        attributeBindings: ['style'],
        style: Ember.computed('size',function() {
          const size = this.get('size');
          return new Ember.Handlebars.SafeString("font-size: "+
            size);
        })

    });
    ```

    All components render as `div` tags inside of templates. We can add different attributes to these `div` tags if needed. In this case, the `attributeBindings` property will add a `style` tag. The `style` tag will be a computed property that updates whenever a `size` value changes. `Ember.Handlebars.SafeString` lets Ember know that the string should be displayed without escaping and that it is safe.

3. Update the `application.hbs` file with the new component:

```
// app/templates/application.hbs
<h2 id="title">Welcome to Ember</h2>

{{#font-sizer size="38px" }}
    Test
{{/font-sizer }}
{{outlet}}
```

The `font-sizer` component is in block form. The test text will be in the `div` block.

4. Update the `font-sizer-test.js` file so that we can check to make sure that the attribute was added:

```
// tests/integration/components/font-sizer-test.js
import { moduleForComponent, test } from 'ember-qunit';
import hbs from 'htmlbars-inline-precompile';

moduleForComponent('font-sizer', 'Integration | Component |
  font sizer', {
    integration: true
});

test('check attributes', function(assert) {

    this.render(hbs`{{font-sizer size=val}}`);
    this.set('val','38px');
    assert.equal(this.$('div').attr('style'),
      'font-size: 38px', 'size is set to 38px');

});
```

This code is automatically generated for us when we created the component. The `moduleForComponent` helper is used for components. The `integration: true` tags this test as an integration test. By doing this, we have the ability to render the component and pass the `size` property to it. The `assert.equal` method is used to check whether `font-size` is set correctly.

5. Run `ember server` and check `/tests`:

The test case passed

Testing actions in the font-sizer component

We can simulate actions and test the results to verify the expected results.

1. Using the existing application, update the `font-sizer.js` file with a new action:

```
// app/components/font-sizer.js
...
    textInfo: 'Hello World',
    }),
    actions: {
      updateText(){
        this.set('textInfo','Hi');
      }
    }

});
```

This new action will set the `textInfo` property to `'Hi'`.

2. Update the `font-sizer.js` file in the `components` folder:

```
// app/templates/components/font-sizer.hbs
<div id='info'>{{textInfo}}</div><br>
{{yield}}<br>
<button {{action 'updateText'}}>Update Text</button>
```

In this template, we created a new `div` tag with an ID of `info` surrounding the `textInfo` property. A new `updateText` action was added to the `button` click. This action updates the `textInfo` property.

3. Add a new test to the `font-sizer-test.js` file so that it can check the new action added:

```
// tests/integration/components/font-sizer-test.js
...
test('check action', function(assert) {

    assert.expect(2);
    this.render(hbs`{{font-sizer}}`);
    assert.equal(this.$('#info').text(), 'Hello World', |
        'starting text is hello world');
    this.$('button').click();
    assert.equal(this.$('#info').text(),
        'Hi', 'text changed   to hi');

});
```

By setting `assert.expect(2)`, the test must have two asserts or it will fail. We first render the component using the `this.render` helper. The next statement checks whether the value returned from `this.$('#info').text()` equals `Hello World`. We then simulate clicking the button. The last statement checks whether `this.$('#info').text()` equals `Hi`.

4. Run `ember server` and navigate to `/tests`. All the tests will pass:

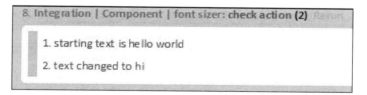

How it works...

Components use integration tests by way of the `moduleForComponent` helper. This feature of Ember's QUnit takes advantage of how Ember actually sees your components. You can test bound values as well as the returning actions.

Testing routes

Testing routes can be done either by acceptance tests or unit tests. In this example, we'll create a simple unit test for a route.

How to do it...

1. In a new application, generate a new `students` route:

   ```
   $ ember g route students
   ```

   This command will generate the route code for students.

2. Edit the students route information and add a new property:

   ```
   // app/routes/students.js
   import Ember from 'ember';

   export default Ember.Route.extend({
       someText: 'someText'
   });
   ```

   This route has a property called `someText`.

3. Edit the `students-tests.js` file in the `tests/unit/routes` folder:

   ```
   // tests/unit/routes/students-test.js
   import { moduleFor, test } from 'ember-qunit';

   moduleFor('route:students', 'Unit | Route | students', {
       // Specify the other units that are required for this
         test.
   });

   test('check prop and route exists', function(assert) {
       let route = this.subject();
       assert.expect(3);
       assert.equal(route.get('someText'),'someText');
       route.set('someText','otherText');
       assert.equal(route.get('someText'),'otherText');
       assert.ok(route);
   });
   ```

In this example, we are checking the output of the `someText` property. The first `assert.equal` gets the property and checks it against the `someText` value. The route instance can also set properties. The next assert checks to see whether the new value has been set. The final assert makes sure that the route is available.

4. Run `ember server` and navigate to `/tests`:

13. Unit | Route | students: check prop and route exists (3) Rerun

1. okay

2. okay

3. okay

This shows all the tests passed

How it works...

The route in your Ember application has a few different functions. It can hold your model data and have properties and actions. When testing routes, we can use it with a more general acceptance test or as an individual unit test.

Testing models

When testing models, you can use Ember Data to help. In this recipe, we'll create a model and test to make sure that it's creating data correctly.

How to do it...

1. In a new application, generate a new student model:

```
$ ember g model student.js
```

This will generate the necessary files for the student model.

2. Update the student model with two properties:

```
// app/models/student.js
import DS from 'ember-data';

export default DS.Model.extend({
    firstName: DS.attr('string'),
    lastName: DS.attr('string')
});
```

This model has two properties, `firstName` and `lastName`. Both hold `string` values.

3. Add a new unit test for the new model that tests the new properties:

```
// tests/unit/models/student-test.js
import { moduleForModel, test } from 'ember-qunit';

moduleForModel('student', 'Unit | Model | student', {
    // Specify the other units that are required for this
      test.
    needs: []
});

test('it exists', function(assert) {
    let model = this.subject();
    assert.ok(!!model);
});

test('Test model data', function(assert) {
    assert.expect(2);
    let model = this.subject({firstName: 'Erik', lastName:
      'Hanchett'});
    assert.equal(model.get('firstName'),
      'Erik', 'first Name is Erik');
    assert.equal(model.get('lastName'),
      'Hanchett', 'last Name is Erik');
});
```

4. This test uses the `moduleForModel` helper. The first test checks whether the model is okay and it exists. The second test checks the properties:

```
...
test('Test model data', function(assert) {
    assert.expect(2);
    let model = this.subject({firstName: 'Erik', lastName:
      'Hanchett'});
    assert.equal(model.get('firstName'),
      'Erik', 'first Name is Erik');
    assert.equal(model.get('lastName'),
      'Hanchett', 'last Name is Erik');
});
```

When creating the `model` instance, you can pass in the values of the `model` properties. In this case, the `{firstName: 'Erik', lastName: 'Hanchett'}` object is created in the store. We can access these values using the `model.get` method. The `assert.equal` method checks against the model to make sure that the values match.

5. Run `ember server` and navigate to `/tests`, and you'll see the passing tests:

> **11. Unit | Model | student: Test model data (2)**
>
> 1. first Name is Erik
>
> 2. last Name is Erik

This shows that both tests passed

How it works...

The `moduleForModel` helper is used to access Ember's model information. This is done with Ember Data so that models can be tested. Ember's QUnit provides a way to test the module completely.

Testing controllers

Controllers should be tested in your application. In this recipe, we'll test some basic actions from a controller.

How to do it...

1. Create a new `index` controller:

   ```
   $ ember g controller index
   ```

   This creates a new controller called `index`.

2. In the index controller, add a new property and action:

   ```
   // app/controllers/index.js
   import Ember from 'ember';

   export default Ember.Controller.extend({
       myValue: 'value',
   ```

```
    actions:{
      pressed(value){
        this.set('myValue',value);
      }
    }
});
```

This controller has one property named `myValue`. Another action called `pressed` changes the value of `myValue` to whatever value is passed in the function.

3. Update the index unit test. Add a few tests for the action and property:

```
// tests/unit/controllers/index-test.js
import { moduleFor, test } from 'ember-qunit';

moduleFor('controller:index', 'Unit | Controller | index',
  {
    // Specify the other units that are required for this
      test.
    // needs: ['controller:foo']
});

// Replace this with your real tests.
test('it exists', function(assert) {
    let controller = this.subject();
    assert.ok(controller);
});

test('check property', function(assert) {
    assert.expect(2);
    let controller = this.subject();
    assert.equal(controller.get('myValue'),'value');
    controller.send('pressed','newValue');
    assert.equal(controller.get('myValue'),'newValue');
});
```

4. The `moduleFor` helper is used here for controllers. The first test checks to make sure that the controller exists:

```
...
test('check property', function(assert) {
    assert.expect(2);
    let controller = this.subject();
    assert.equal(controller.get('myValue'),'value');
    controller.send('pressed','newValue');
    assert.equal(controller.get('myValue'),'newValue');
});
```

This test creates an instance of the controller with `this.subject`. The initial value is checked to make sure that it's correct. To send an action to the controller, the `controller.send` method is called. The send method can take one or more parameters. The first is the name of the action to be triggered. This is followed by any values that should be passed in the method.

5. Run `ember server` and navigate to `/tests`. This will display the passed tests:

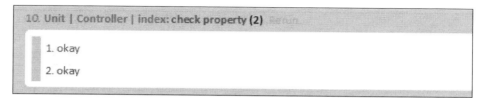

This message shows that all tests passed

How it works...

Controller tests are very similar to the unit tests that we discussed before. They use QUnit's `moduleFor` helper. In a controller, we can test the properties or actions and make sure that the results are as we expected.

9
Real-Life Tasks
with Ember.js

In this chapter, we'll cover the following recipes:

- ▶ Using services with a component
- ▶ Managing basic authentication
- ▶ Using **OAuth2** with Ember Simple Auth
- ▶ Using Liquid Fire to create transitions
- ▶ Working with HTML5 drag and drop
- ▶ Learning Bootstrap with Ember.js

Introduction

When developing a web application, you'll run into some tricky situations. You might need to set up authentication or animations or add transitions. You may need to figure out how to use Bootstrap in your application. These scenarios happen all the time.

In this chapter, we'll go over some more common real-life tasks and some recipes that you can use to make life easier when working with Ember.js.

Using services with a component

In Ember.js, a service is a singleton object that holds state. In other words, it can be shared throughout an Ember application and doesn't change. For example, session data, APIs that talk to a server, and **WebSockets** are good candidates for services.

In this recipe, we'll create and inject a service into a component.

> **Dependency injection**
>
> Services and dependency injection go hand in hand. **Dependency Injection** (**DI**) occurs when we take objects and inject them into other objects during instantiation. This means that we take a service and inject it into our routes, controllers, and components. This is an important framework concept and should not be overused. Having too many injected services would break the separation of concerns design principle.

How to do it...

1. In a new application, generate these files:

    ```
    $ ember g service start
    $ ember g component comp-info
    $ ember g initializer init
    ```

    These files will be used to create our application. The service will hold a property and method that returns data.

2. Begin by editing the `start.js` service:

    ```
    // app/services/start.js
    import Ember from 'ember';

    export default Ember.Service.extend({
        isOn: false,
        importantInfo(){
          return "Important Info is " + this.get('isOn');
        }
    });
    ```

    This is the `services` file. It has an `isOn` property and a method called `importantInfo` that returns a string. In this example, we want access to this information in our component, `comp-info`, so that it can be displayed.

3. Edit the component `comp-info.js` file and add a new action that uses the `start` services information:

```
// app/components/comp-info.js
import Ember from 'ember';

export default Ember.Component.extend({
    start: Ember.inject.service(),
    message: null,
    actions: {
      pressMe() {
        this.start.toggleProperty('isOn');
        this.set('message',this.start.importantInfo());
        console.log(this.start.isOn);
      }
    }

});
```

The most important thing in the component is the `start` property. We can inject the `start` service into the component using `Ember.inject.service()`. By convention, the name of the property must match the name of the service being injected. In our example, the `start` service will be injected.

The `pressMe` action toggles the `isOn` property of the `start` service. We then set the text returned from the `importantInfo` method in the `message` property so that it can be displayed in the template.

4. Add `button` to the template information for the component:

```
// app/templates/components/comp-info.hbs
<button {{action "pressMe"}}>push me</button><br>
{{message}}
```

In the component, all we are doing is adding an action to the button and displaying a message.

5. Add the `comp-info` component to the application template file:

```
<h2 id="title">Welcome to Ember</h2>

{{outlet}}
{{comp-info}}
```

Now the template will display the component that was just created.

6. Start the Ember server, and it will look as follows:

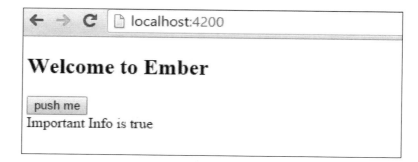

Pressing the button will toggle the isOn property. As you can see from this example, the service information was accessed by the component and displayed to the template.

7. Create initializer that injects the service into all the components:

```
// app/initializer/init
export function initialize(app) {
    app.inject('component', 'start', 'service:start');
}

export default {
    name: 'init',
    initialize
};
```

Ember.js initializers are created when the application is started. It's a good place to preload data or set up the application state. The app argument, in the initialize function, is also known as Ember.Application. It serves as a registry for dependency declaration. Factories (classes) can be registered and injected into the application. The service:start is the key for the start service that we created earlier. Once a factory is registered, it can be injected anywhere in the application. As the start service has already been created, there is no need to register it.

The app.inject takes three arguments. The first is the type to be injected. The second is the name of the service, start. Finally, the service:start factory is created.

8. Update the component so that it no longer injects the `start` service as it's already available via the dependency injection:

```
// app/components/comp-info.js
...
export default Ember.Component.extend({
    //start: Ember.inject.service(),
    message: null,
...
```

The `start` service is commented out so it's no longer available. The rest of the component remains the same as the service can still be retrieved using `this.get('start')`. This is due to the fact that we injected it into all the components in the initializer.

9. Run the server again and the template loaded will remain the same with the same functionality.

How it works...

Services are long-lived Ember objects that can be used in different parts of your application. They are good to use with sessions, WebSockets, geolocation, logging, and more. They can be made available to the rest of the application using `Ember.inject.service`, which is a method that can retrieve services and make them available.

DI can be used to inject services into many different parts of the Ember application. Ember's architecture uses factories that are registered by `Ember.Application`. We can inject into all routes, components, and controllers using the `Application.inject` method.

Managing basic authentication

In any real-world Ember application, at some point, you'll need to deal with authentication. For example, users might need to send their credentials to identify themselves to the server, or authenticated users may need access to protected parts of the application.

An important aspect of authentication is protecting information based on the logged in user. This can be done by creating sessions with the use of tokens. In this recipe, we'll create a simple token-based authentication with an Express server. This will help us understand the basics. In the next section, we'll go over using OAuth2 with Ember Simple Auth.

How to do it...

1. In a new application, generate these files:

```
$ ember g service session
$ ember g adapter application
$ ember g controller login
$ ember g model student name:string age:number
$ ember g route login
$ ember g route students
$ ember g template index
$ ember g server index
$ npm install body-parser -save-dev
```

This will generate all the scaffolding that we need for our application. The `students` route will be protected. It will only populate information from the server if the user is authenticated.

The `ember g server index` command will generate a node Express mock server for us. In the previous chapters, we used Ember CLI Mirage to do all our mock tests. The Express server generated by Ember is not as powerful. However, it will be easier to set up our fake server and authentication example. Be aware that when deploying an Ember application to production, the Ember server will not be included. It will, however, automatically start when running the `ember serve` command.

2. Create a new service called session that will handle our authentication and keep track of authenticated users:

```
// app/services/session.js
import Ember from 'ember';

export default Ember.Service.extend({
    token: null,
    authenticate(log, pass) {
      return Ember.$.ajax({
        method: 'POST',
        url: '/token',
        data: { username: log, password: pass}
      }).then((info)=>{
        this.set('token',info.access_token);
      });
    }

});
```

This service will be injected into our login controller. This will keep track of authenticated users and send Ajax requests to the server. The `authenticate` method accepts the login name and password. These values are sent to the server using an HTTP `POST` method to `/token`. If the login information is correct, a token is returned and saved. If not, an error will be returned. We'll deal with the error in the login controller later.

The `token` property will be used to keep track whether the user is authenticated or not.

3. Update the Express server `index.js` file. Add a route for `token`:

```
// server/index.js
/*jshint node:true*/

const bodyParser = require('body-parser');


module.exports = function(app) {
    app.post('/token', function(req, res) {

      if (req.body.username === 'erik' &&
        req.body.password === 'password') {
        res.send({ access_token: "secretcode" });
      } else {
        res.status(400).send({ error: "invalid_grant" });
      }

    });
};
```

This is our node Express server. It will run when we start the Ember server. When the HTTP `POST` `/token` request is sent to the server, it will check the body `username` and `password`. For this example, we'll just hardcode them as `'erik'` and `'secretcode'`. If these match, it returns `access_token`. If not, it returns an invalid message.

The access token will be saved in the session service. We can use this token to authenticate future requests to the server.

4. Update the `application.js` file. Add a new authorization header:

```
// app/adapters/application.js
import DS from 'ember-data';
import Ember from 'ember';
```

```
export default DS.RESTAdapter.extend({
    namespace: 'api',
    session: Ember.inject.service(),
    headers: Ember.computed('session.token',function(){
      return {
        'Authorization': `Bearer
           ${this.get('session.token')}`
      };
    })
});
```

In our application, accessing the students route will trigger a request to the server. The server will respond to authenticated users only. The server expects an authorization bearer header with every Ember Data request. We can do this using the `headers computed` property and returning the `Authorization: Bearer` header with the secret token from the service. Every request to the server, using Ember Data, will send this header.

5. Update the Express server index information in order to return information to the application if the token matches:

```
// app/server/index.js
...
    app.use(bodyParser.urlencoded({ extended: true }));

    app.get('/api/students', function (req, res) {

      if (req.headers.authorization !== "Bearer
        secretcode") {
        return res.status(401).send('Unauthorized');
      }

      return res.status(200).send({
        students: [
          { id: 1, name: 'Erik', age: 24 },
          { id: 2, name: 'Suze', age: 32 },
          { id: 3, name: 'Jill', age: 18 }
        ]

      });
    });
...
```

Above `app.post`, you can add `app.get` for the `students` route. Ember will trigger this HTTP GET request whenever it enters the `/students` route. The server will check whether the request header has the secret code. If it matches, it returns the proper JSON data for the `students` route. If not, it returns a 401 error.

6. Verify the route and model information for students:

```
// app/models/student.js
import DS from 'ember-data';

export default DS.Model.extend({
    name: DS.attr('string'),
    age: DS.attr('number')
});
```

7. Earlier, we generated this file with two properties, `name` and `age`:

```
// app/routes/students.js
import Ember from 'ember';

export default Ember.Route.extend({
    model() {
        return this.store.findAll('student');
    }
});
```

8. The students route will send an HTTP GET request to `/students` to retrieve the students model. As we defined the application to use the REST adapter, Ember will expect the data in the REST format:

```
// app/templates/students.hbs
Secret Student Information
{{#each model as |student|}}
    {{student.name}}<br>
    {{student.age}}<br>
{{/each}}
```

The students template uses the `each` helper to iterate through the model returned from the server. It displays each `name` and `age`.

9. Add the login username and property information to the login template:

```
// app/templates/login.hbs
<h3>Login</h3>

{{input value=loginName placeholder='Login'}}<br>
{{input value=password placeholder='Password'
  type='password'}}<br>
<button {{action 'authenticate'}}>Login</button>
```

This template uses the `input` helper for the `loginName` and `password` properties. The button triggers the `authenticate` action.

10. Update the login controller to handle the `authenticate` action:

```
// app/controllers/login.js
import Ember from 'ember';

export default Ember.Controller.extend({
    loginName: null,
    password: null,
    session: Ember.inject.service(),
    actions: {
      authenticate(){
        this.get('session').authenticate(this.get
          ('loginName'), this.get('password')).then( ()=>{
          alert('Great you are logged in!');
          this.transitionToRoute('students');
        }, (err)=>{
          alert('Error! Problem with token! '+
            err.responseText);
        });
      }
    }
});
```

The controller has several properties. It retrieves the session information service and uses the `authenticate` method to send the login information to the server. The `authenticate` method returns a promise. If it's successful, the application transitions to the `students` route. If it's not successful, an error is displayed in an alert box. In this example, we are using the ES6 arrow function. The `()=>` arrow function is a little shorter than using a function expression and it also lexically binds this variable.

11. Update the index with a link to log in:

```
// app/templates/index.hbs
Welcome to my app! Login {{#link-to 'login'}}here
  {{/link-to}}
```

This is just a simple link to the login route.

12. Start the server and navigate to the login route. You'll see the following image:

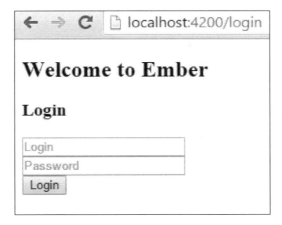

13. To log in, enter the username `'erik'` and password `'password'`. After clicking `Login`, an HTTP POST request will be sent to the server with the name and password information. The Express server that we had set up earlier will respond with the token, and the session service will save it. The application will then transition to the students route. The following screen will be displayed:

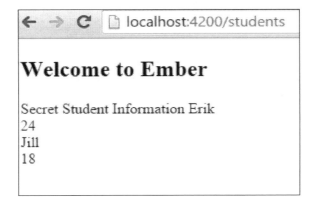

14. When this route loads, an HTTP GET request will be sent to `/students`. The Express server will check to make sure that the authorization bearer header has the correct secret code. It then will respond with the JSON data that Ember will display.

15. If the username or password does not match, the following alert box will be displayed:

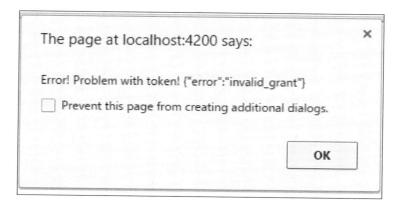

How it works...

Token-based authentication requires the client to send over credentials to the server. If authorized, the server then sends back a token that the client saves and uses on subsequent requests to the server. If the token is not present, the server may not return data to the client.

This recipe is a simple example of using authentication. It lacks proper error handling and session persistence. Nevertheless, it gives you an idea of how authentication works.

Using OAuth2 with Ember Simple Auth

OAuth2 specifies authorization flows for web applications. We can use it with Ember to secure our application and provide data to only those users that are authorized. In this recipe, we'll look at using OAuth2 with **Ember Simple Auth** (**ESA**), a robust add-on for Ember.

ESA will handle our client-side session and authentication and send the requests to the server. It's very customizable and extensible. Although it can be complicated, just like our last recipe, we'll create a protected students route that can be accessed by authorized users only.

Getting ready

For the purposes of this example, we'll need an OAuth2 server. Setting up an OAuth2 server is beyond the scope of this recipe. There are several OAuth2 libraries out there that you can use to set one up. I recommend the following:

- **Rails**: https://github.com/doorkeeper-gem/doorkeeper
- **Express**: https://github.com/thomseddon/node-oauth2-server

How to do it...

1. In a new Ember application, run the generator command to create the required files:

    ```
    $ ember g adapter application
    $ ember g component login-comp
    $ ember g controller login
    $ ember g controller students
    $ ember g model student name:string age:number
    $ ember g route students
    $ ember g route application
    $ ember g route login
    $ ember g template index
    $ ember install ember-simple-auth
    ```

    This will generate the scaffolding that we need to begin our application. The last command installs the add-on for ESA.

2. We'll begin by setting up the Ember Simple Auth authenticator and authorizer for OAuth2. We need to set this up so that a user can authenticate with the server. Create two new directories in the `app` folder called `authenticators` and `authorizers`.

3. Add a new file called `oauth2-custom.js` to the `authenticators` directory and `application.js` to the `authorizers` folder. Add this code:

    ```
    // app/authenticators/oauth2-custom.js
    import Authenticator from 'ember-simple-auth/authenticators/
    oauth2-password-grant';
    import Ember from 'ember';

    export default Authenticator.extend({
        makeRequest(url, data) {

            var client_id = '123';
            var client_secret = 'secret';
            data.grant_type = 'password';

            return Ember.$.ajax({
              url: this.serverTokenEndpoint,
              type: 'POST',
              data: data,
              dataType: 'json',
    ```

```
          contentType: 'application/x-www-form-urlencoded',
          crossDomain: true,
          headers: {
            Authorization: "Basic " +
              btoa(client_id + ":" + client_secret)
          }
        });
      }
    });
```

The `authenticators` file is used by ESA whenever a user logs in. We can overwrite anything in the authenticator if needed. The `makeRequest` method is used to send messages to the server. By default, ESA will make an HTTP POST request to `/token` with the username and password in the form field.

4. Unfortunately, many OAuth2 servers require a header called `Authorization Basic` with a secret client ID and client secret when authenticating for the first time with a server. To fix this, we can extend the `makeRequest` method with our own Ajax request. This will be used when we log in:

```
// app/authorizers/application.js
import OAuth2Bearer from 'ember-simple-auth/authorizers/oauth2-
  bearer';


export default OAuth2Bearer.extend();
```

The `authorizers` file is used by ESA to tell which type of authentication we are using. In this example, we are using Oauth2 as defined by `OAuth2Bearer.extend()`.

5. Update the adapter and add the ESA data adapter mixin to the `application.js` file in the `adapters` folder:

```
// app/adapters/application.js
import DS from 'ember-data';

import DataAdapterMixin from 'ember-simple-auth/mixins/
  data-adapter-mixin';


export default DS.RESTAdapter.extend(DataAdapterMixin, {
    namespace: 'api',
    authorizer: 'authorizer:application'
});
```

The adapter tells Ember to make all requests to the /api namespace. The ESA DataAdapterMixin is used to define the authorizer that the application will use. In this case, all Ember Data requests will use the OAuth2 application authorizer that we defined earlier. In other words, any request sent to the server using Ember Data will include the session data token, if it exists.

6. Let's update our login-comp component template:

```
// app/templates/components/login-comp.hbs
<h2>Login page</h2>

<form {{action 'authenticate' on='submit'}}>
    {{input value=login placeholder='Login'}}<br>
    {{input value=password placeholder='Password'
      type='password'}}<br>
    <button type="submit">Login</button>
</form>
```

This will submit the login and password to the authenticate action setup in our component.

7. Update the login page component with the authenticate action:

```
// app/components/login-comp.js
import Ember from 'ember';

export default Ember.Component.extend({

    auth: Ember.inject.service('session'),
    login: null,
    password: null,
    actions: {
      authenticate() {
        this.get('auth').authenticate
          ('authenticator:oauth2-custom', this.get('login'),
            this.get('password')).then(() => {
          alert('Thanks for logging in!');
          this.get('transition')();
          }, () => {
            alert('Wrong user name or password!');
          });
        }
    }

});
```

As we are using ESA, we have access to a `session` service. This `session` service has an `authenticate` method that uses `authenticator` that we created earlier. In the preceding code, we used the `this.get()` method to get `login` and `password` from our template. We then called the `authenticate` method on our service, passing in our `authenticator`.

If the server returns a successful message, then we call `transition`, a method that is passed to the component. If not, an alert box pops up telling the user that their login was not successful.

8. Add the login page component to the login template, and update the login controller:

```
// app/templates/login.hbs
{{login-comp transition=(action 'loggedIn')}}
```

This calls the login component and passes in the parent action, `loggedIn`:

```
// app/controllers/login.js
import Ember from 'ember';

export default Ember.Controller.extend({
    actions: {
      loggedIn(){
        this.transitionToRoute('students');
      }
    }
});
```

This action transitions the application to the `students` route. It's triggered only with a successful login. It's also the name of the action passed in the login page component.

9. Update the students controller, route, and template:

```
// app/templates/students.hbs
<h2>Students</h2>
{{#each model as |student|}}
    <h3>Student: {{student.name}} </h3>
    <h3>Age: {{student.age}} </h3>
{{/each}}


<button {{action 'logout'}}>Log Out</button>
```

The template displays the information from the server using the `each` helper. A `logout` button action will log the user out:

```
// app/controllers/students.js
import Ember from 'ember';

export default Ember.Controller.extend({
    auth: Ember.inject.service('session'),
    actions: {
      logout(){
        this.get('auth').invalidate();
      }
    }
});
```

10. The `logout` action invalidates the session. Invalidating the session revokes the token so that it is no longer available:

```
// app/routes/students.js
import Ember from 'ember';
import AuthenticatedRouteMixin from 'ember-simple-auth/mixins/
authenticated-route-mixin';

export default Ember.Route.extend(AuthenticatedRouteMixin,{
    model(){
      return this.store.findAll('student');
    }
});
```

This route returns all the information for the `student` model. You'll notice that `AuthenticatedRouteMixin` is added. This tells Ember to make this route available only if it's authenticated by the server. If it's not, it will route back to the application.

11. Add the application mixin to the application route:

```
// app/routes/application.js
import Ember from 'ember';

import ApplicationRouteMixin from 'ember-simple-
  auth/mixins/application-route-mixin';

export default Ember.Route.extend(ApplicationRouteMixin);
```

ESA's `ApplicationRouteMixin` will catch any errors and transition to the login route.

12. Update the index template with a link to the login route:

```
// app/templates/index.hbs
Hello! Want to login? Click {{#link-to
    'login'}}here!{{/link-to}}
```

The `link-to` helper links to the `login` route.

13. Start the Ember server and OAuth2 server:

```
$ ember serve --proxy http://localhost:3000
```

The `--proxy` argument tells Ember to proxy all server requests to `localhost` at port `3000`. We'll assume, in this example, that the OAuth2 server is running on port `3000` in your local box.

A successful login will look like this:

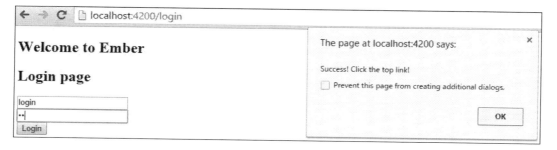

It will then redirect to the students route. This route will send a request to the server with an authorization bearer request with the correct token. It will receive the student data so that it can be displayed to the user:

Accessing this route without being logged in causes redirection to the login page.

How it works...

The Ember Simple Auth add-on manages the session, authentication, authorization, persistence, and communication with a server. It has its own built-in session service that makes it easy to manage.

OAuth2 is a specification of a type of flow when doing authentication in web apps. As Ember is a single-page application, there is not much security on the application side. It must rely on a server to authenticate and manage tokens. ESA makes this possible by handling all the work needed to send and communicate with the server.

Using Liquid Fire to create transitions

Ember Liquid Fire is an add-on for Ember that handles animations and transitions. It's a toolkit of sorts that splits its responsibilities between template headers, transition maps, and transitions.

In this recipe, we'll create a few transitions to see how this add-on works.

How to do it...

1. In a new Ember application, generate these files:

   ```
   $ ember g route tut1
   $ ember g route tut2
   $ ember g template index
   $ ember install liquid-fire
   ```

   This will generate the scaffolding for the `tut1` and `tut2` routes as well as install the `liquid-fire` add-on.

2. Create a new `transitions.js` file in the root of the `app` folder. Add a few transitions:

   ```
   // app/transitions.js
   export default function(){
       this.transition(
         this.fromRoute('tut1'),
         this.toRoute('tut2'),
         this.use('toRight'),
         this.reverse('toLeft')
   ```

```
);
this.transition(
  this.fromRoute('index'),
  this.toRoute('tut1'),
  this.use('crossFade'),
  this.reverse('fade',{duration: 500})

);

}
```

Liquid Fire requires a transitions map file. There are a number of predefined transitions that you have available:

- toLeft
- toRight
- toUp
- toDown
- crossFade
- fade

Each one behaves as you would expect. The `toLeft` transition will create a transition animation where the page moves from left to right. The `toRight` transition is the exact opposite. You can also create your own animations if needed.

The map tells us which transitions to use when moving from one route to another.

3. Update the application template with the Liquid Fire outlet:

```
// app/templates/application.hbs
{{#link-to 'application'}}<h2 id="title">Welcome to
  Ember</h2>{{/link-to}}
{{liquid-outlet}}
```

To use Liquid Fire transitions, we must use `liquid-outlet`. This is used when transitioning between routes. Here are all the template helpers available:

- `{{#liquid-outlet}}`: This transitions between routes
- `{{#liquid-with}}`: This transitions between models or contexts in a single route
- `{{#liquid-bind}}`: This updates to simple bound values
- `{{#liquid-if}}`: This switches between true and false branches in a `#if` statement

- ❑ `{{#liquid-spacer}}`: This provides a smoothly growing/shrinking container that animates whenever the contained **Document Object Model (DOM)** mutates

4. In the index template file, add a link to the `tut1` route:

```
// app/templates/index.hbs
{{#link-to 'tut1'}}First Transition{{/link-to}}<br>
{{liquid-outlet}}
```

The `link-to` helper transitions to the `tut1` route. The liquid outlet will display the `tut1` route when it renders.

5. Update the `tut1` and `tut2` route templates:

```
// app/templates/tut1.hbs
{{#link-to 'tut2'}}Tutorial 2{{/link-to}}<br>
<div class="demo">
    <p>
    Lorem ipsum dolor sit amet, consectetur adipiscing elit.
      In non aliquet quam. Vivamus egestas mi sapien, augue.
    </p>
</div>

{{liquid-outlet}}
```

All this does is have a link to the second route `tut2`:

```
// app/templates/tut2
{{#link-to 'tut1'}}Tutorial 1{{/link-to}}<br>

<div class='demo'>
<p>
Quisque molestie libero vel tortor viverra. Quisque eu posuere
sem. Aenean ut arcu quam. Morbi orci dui, dictum ut libero
in, venenatis tempor nulla. Nullam convallis mauris ante, sed
venenatis augue auctor in. Morbi a mi a sapien dictum interdum.
Quisque faucibus malesuada risus eget pretium. Ut elementum sapien
ut nunc eleifend, at dapibus enim dignissim.
</p>
</div>
{{liquid-outlet}}
```

This has a link back to `tut1`.

6. Run the server and you'll see the transitions as you click on the links:

This is what it looks like mid-transition using crossfade from the application route to the `tut1` route.

How it works...

Liquid Fire is a versatile add-on for Ember that brings transitions and animation to life. It uses a simple transition map and template helpers to make things easier. Under the hood, Liquid Fire uses many tricks to make these animations possible. It's extensible, so you can create your own transitions as well.

Working with HTML5 drag and drop

Drag and drop is a part of the HTML5 standard. It allows the user to grab objects in the DOM and drop them at different locations. Any element can be draggable if the browser supports it. Most modern browsers do.

In this recipe, we'll see an example of dragging an IMG file to a drop zone on the screen.

How to do it...

1. In a new application, generate these files:

```
$ ember g component drag-drop-zone
$ ember g component drag-drop
```

The `drag-drop-zone` component will represent the area where each item will be dropped. The `drag-drop` component will be the item to be dropped.

2. Edit the `drag-drop-zone.js` file:

```
// app/components/drag-drop-zone.js
import Ember from 'ember';

export default Ember.Component.extend({
    classNames: ['draggable-dropzone'],
    classNameBindings: ['dragClass'],
    dragClass: 'deactivated',
    dragLeave(event) {
      event.preventDefault();
      return this.set('dragClass', 'deactivated');
    },
    dragOver(event) {
      event.preventDefault();
      return this.set('dragClass', 'activated');
    },
    drop(event) {
      var data;
      this.set('dragClass', 'deactivated');
      data = event.dataTransfer.getData('text/data');
      event.target.appendChild
        (document.getElementById(data));
    }

});
```

This component has a few special events attached to it. Ember has built-in events for `dragLeave`, `dragOver`, and `drop`. These will fire whenever items are dragged on top of the component. Remember that all components render as `div` tags. We can use the `classNames` property to add more classes.

The `classNameBindings` property allows classes to be added to the component as if they were properties. In other words, `dragClass` can be set dynamically in the component. We'll use this to change the color of the `drop` zone when items are dragged over it. When items are dropped, the `drop` event is triggered.

3. Update the drag drop component:

```
// app/components/drag-drop.js
import Ember from 'ember';

export default Ember.Component.extend({
    tagName: 'img',
    classNames: ['draggable-item'],
```

```
            attributeBindings: ['draggable','src'],
            draggable: 'true',
            src: 'http://www.programwitherik.com/content/images/
              2015/02/eriksmall3-1.png ',
            dragStart(event){
              event.dataTransfer.setData('text/data',
                event.target.id);
            }
    });
```

As mentioned earlier, normally, components render as a `div` tag. However, we can change this using the `tagName` property. In the `drag-drop` component, we are creating an `image` tag. The `dragStart` event available in Ember. In this example, we are setting the data to the target ID.

To drag items in HTML5, you must have a `draggable` attribute on the tag. It also must be set to `true`. We'll use `attributeBindings` to make this possible.

4. Update the `app.css` file:

```
// app/styles/app.css
.draggable-dropzone {
    border: 1px solid black;
    width: 200px;
    height:200px;


}

.activated {
    border: 4px solid red;
}
```

This is some basic `css` that creates a border around the `drop` zone and changes the color to `red` when an item is about to be dropped.

5. The last step is to add the components to the application template file:

```
// app/templates/application.hbs
<h2 id="title">Welcome to Ember</h2>

<br>
{{drag-drop-zone}}

<br>
<br>
<br>
{{drag-drop}}
{{outlet}}
```

This will render the two components to the application template.

6. Render the page and you'll see the picture and dropzone:

You can drag the picture into the box:

The box will turn red before the item is dropped and back to black after it's dropped.

How it works...

The HTML5 standard allows dragging and dropping elements. Ember has several built-in events that we can use in components and controllers. The `dragLeave`, `dragOver`, `drop`, and `dragStart` methods can all be used to capture events to allow dragging and dropping.

Learning Bootstrap with Ember.js

Bootstrap, formerly known as Twitter Bootstrap, is a popular, free, and open source collection of tools to create websites and applications. It contains several templates for typography, forms, buttons, and navigation.

You can use Bootstrap to make nice and simple user interfaces. In this recipe, we'll use it to create a drop-down menu.

How to do it...

1. In a new Ember application, use Bower to install the latest version of Bootstrap:

```
$ bower install bootstrap --save-dev
```

This uses Bower's frontend package manager to install Bootstrap. It will be saved as a development dependency in the `bower.json` file.

2. Update the `ember-cli-build.js` file and add the libraries for Ember Bootstrap:

```
// ember-cli-build.js
/* global require, module */
var EmberApp = require('ember-cli/lib/broccoli/ember-app');

module.exports = function(defaults) {
    var app = new EmberApp(defaults, {
      // Add options here
    });

    app.import('bower_components/
      bootstrap/dist/js/bootstrap.js');
    app.import('bower_components/
      bootstrap/dist/css/bootstrap.css');
    return app.toTree();
};
```

The `app.import` statement takes the asset path as the first and only argument. This is standard for non-AMD assets. Once this is loaded, we can use Bootstrap anywhere in our application.

3. Add a drop-down button to the application template:

```
// app/templates/application.hbs
<h2 id="title">Welcome to Ember</h2>

{{outlet}}

<!-- Single button -->
<div class="btn-group">
<button type="button" class="btn btn-default dropdown-toggle"
data-toggle="dropdown" aria-haspopup="true" aria-expanded="false">
Action <span class="caret"></span>
</button>
<ul class="dropdown-menu">
<li><a href="#">Action</a></li>
<li><a href="#">Another action</a></li>
<li><a href="#">Something else here</a></li>
<li role="separator" class="divider"></li>
<li><a href="#">Separated link</a></li>
</ul>
</div>
```

This will add a drop-down button.

4. Start the server and you'll see the rendered button:

After clicking on the button, the menu will be displayed.

5. Let's install the Bootstrap Ember add-on and comment out `app.imports` in the `ember-cli-build.js` file:

```
$ ember install ember-bootstrap
```

Ember Bootstrap is an add-on that includes all the normal `css` and icon assets in your project. It also includes a set of native Ember components. It does not use the Bootstrap JavaScript file:

```
// ember-cli-build.js

...

//app.import('bower_components/bootstrap/dist/js/bootstrap.js');

//app.import('bower_components/bootstrap/dist/css/bootstrap.css');

...
```

As we are using the add-on, we must comment out the Bootstrap files. They are already included.

6. Update the application template file using the new Ember Bootstrap components:

```
// app/templates/application.hbs
<h2 id="title">Welcome to Ember</h2>

<nav class="navbar navbar-default navbar-static">
    <div class="container-fluid">
      <ul class="nav navbar-nav">
        {{#bs-dropdown tagName="li"}}
        {{#bs-dropdown-toggle}}Example Dropdown <span
        class="caret"></span>{{/bs-dropdown-toggle}}
          {{#bs-dropdown-menu}}
            <li>{{#link-to "info1"}}Info 1{{/link-to}}</li>
            <li>{{#link-to "info2"}}Info 2{{/link-to}}</li>
          {{/bs-dropdown-menu}}
        {{/bs-dropdown}}
      </ul>
    </div>
</nav>

{{outlet}}
```

All the Ember Bootstrap components start with `bs`. The `{{bs-dropdown}}` component creates a drop-down menu that displays links to the user.

Using Ember Bootstrap can be a little cleaner and easier than installing Bootstrap with Bower.

7. Load the server and you'll see the following image:

This is using Ember Bootstrap to create a menu.

How it works...

Bootstrap is a versatile set of tools that can help you design a frontend quickly. Ember accepts assets using a library called Broccoli. Broccoli is an asset pipeline—it helps build the application. The `app.import` statement is used to bring AMD and non-AMD assets in the application.

On the other hand, the Ember Bootstrap library can also be used. It has easy-to-use components built-in that make it easy to add buttons and menus.

10
Awesome Tasks with Ember

In this chapter, we'll cover the following recipes:

- ► Using Ember validations
- ► Using D3.js with Ember.js
- ► Using Ember with Sockets
- ► Using Ember with Firebase
- ► Using server-side rendering

Introduction

In this chapter, you'll learn everything from validating form data to looking at Ember's server-side rendering. Each recipe will show you the power and possibilities that Ember gives to create ambitious applications.

Using Ember validations

Data form validation is a very common use case in web development. The end user will know immediately if they've made a mistake when you create validation rules in your application.

In this recipe, we'll take a look at two examples on validation. In the first example, we'll use a component and check data based on a few simple validation rules. In the second example, we'll use a popular Ember add-on to make things easier.

How to do it...

1. In a new application, create two components and install the validation add-on:

   ```
   $ ember g component val-example
   $ ember g component val-example2
   $ ember install ember-cp-validations
   ```

   The `val-example` component will be the first example. The `val-example2` component will be the second example using the `ember-cp-validations` add-on.

2. Update the `val-example.hbs` component template file:

   ```
   // app/templates/components/val-example.hbs
   Enter Age:<br>
   {{input value=num}}
   <button {{action 'check'}}>Check</button><br>
   {{error}}<br>
   ```

   This component asks for an age. If the button is clicked, the `'check'` action will be triggered. A simple `input` helper is used to capture the input. The `{{error}}` property displays the error text.

3. In the `val-example.js` component file, add a `check` action and simple `validation` method:

   ```
   // app/components/val-example.js
   import Ember from 'ember';

   export default Ember.Component.extend({
       num: null,
       actions:{
         check(){
           if(this.validation(this.get('num'))){
             this.set('error','');
           }
           else{
             this.set('error','Error in box!');
           }

           console.log(this.getProperties('num'));
         }
       },
       validation(value){
         return Number(parseInt(value))==value;
       }

   });
   ```

The `check` action calls the `validation` method. The `validation` method's only purpose is to return `true` if the value is a number and return `false` if the value is not. This result is used to set the `error` property that will be used in the template.

This is a fairly simple example. It shows what you might need to validate the field. Another example might be creating a new computed property and have it depend on the `num` property. Either way will work.

4. Add the component to the `application.hbs` template file:

```
// app/templates/application.hbs
<h2 id="title">Welcome to Ember</h2>

{{outlet}}

{{val-example}}
```

The `val-example` component will render at `{{val-example}}`.

5. Run `ember server` and enter a non-numeric value in the textbox. The following window will be displayed:

The **Error in box!** message is displayed because a number was not entered. This was triggered after the **Check** button was clicked.

For the next example, we'll use an Ember add-on instead.

6. Update the `val-example2.hbs` template file so that it can accept an e-mail and number:

```
// app/templates/components/val-example2.hbs
Enter Age:<br>
{{input value=num}}<br>
    <div style='color: red'>
      {{message}}<br>
    </div>
```

```
Enter Email:<br>
{{input value=email}}<br>
    <div style='color: red'>
      {{emailMessage}}<br>
    </div>
<button {{action 'check'}}>Check</button><br>
```

This second component is a little more complicated than the first. We'll be validating two form fields, a number field and e-mail field. In addition, we'll be surrounding the message in a `div` tag that will be used to help set `color` of the text. Both fields will be validated after pressing the `check` button.

7. Create a new `validations.js` file in the `components` folder:

```
// app/components/validations.js
import { validator, buildValidations } from 'ember-cp-
validations';

export default buildValidations({
    num: [
    validator('number',{
      allowString: true,
      integer: true,
      message: 'Error! This is not an integer!'
    }),
    validator('presence', true)
    ],
    email: [
      validator('format', {
        type: 'email',
        message: 'This is not an email address!'
      }),
    ],
});
```

This file is needed for the `ember-cp-validations` add-on. In this file, we define our validation rules. We begin by naming each property and defining the validations needed. We can validate many different types of inputs. A list of these validations can be found at `http://offirgolan.github.io/ember-cp-validations/docs/index.html`.

The `validator` add-on comes with several prebuilt messages. We can overwrite these messages by setting the `message` property. In the preceding code, the `num` and `email` validators have custom messages. The `num` validator checks to see whether any value is in the field and whether it's a number. The e-mail field checks to see whether the value is in the format of an e-mail address.

8. Add a new `check` action to the component:

```
// app/components/val-example2.js
Import Ember from 'ember';
import Validations from './validations';

export default Ember.Component.extend(Validations,{
    num: null,
      email: null,
      message: '',
      emailMessage: '',
      actions: {
        check(){
          this.set('message','');
          this.set('emailMessage','');
          this.validate().then(({model, validations})=>{

            if(validations.get('isValid')){
              this.set('message','');
              this.set('emailMessage','');
            }
            else{

              if(model.get
                ('validations.attrs.num.isInvalid')){
                this.set('message',model.get
                  ('validations.attrs.num.messages'));
              }
              if(model.get
                ('validations.attrs.email.isInvalid')){
                this.set('emailMessage',model.get
                  ('validations.attrs.email.messages'));
              }
            }

          },(errors)=>{
            console.log(errors);
          });

        }
      }
});
```

9. After setting up the `validations` file, you can add it to the component as a mixin. After adding the `validations` mixin, you'll have access to the `validate()` method. This is a promise that returns after it validates the fields:

```
...
    this.validate().then(({model, validations})=>{

      if(validations.get('isValid')){
        this.set('message','');
        this.set('emailMessage','');
      }
...
```

The `validations` have an `isValid` property. This will only return `true` if both properties, `num` and `email`, passed `validation`.

10. We can check each individual validation as well:

```
...
 else{

    if(model.get('validations.attrs.num.isInvalid')){
      this.set('message',model.get
        ('validations.attrs.num.messages'));
    }
    if(model.get('validations.attrs.email.isInvalid')){
      this.set('emailMessage',model.get
        ('validations.attrs.email.messages'));
...
```

We can access the `model` properties in the component. This `model` will have both the `num` and email `properties`. We can use `validations.attrs.num.isInvalid` to check whether the validation failed. If it did, we can set `message` we created earlier with `validations.attrs.num.messages`.

In the preceding code, if the validation is not valid, then we set the error message that will be displayed in the template after the `check` action is triggered.

This add-on is very flexible. We can create our own custom validations if needed.

11. Update the `application.hbs` file with the second component:

```
// app/templates/application.hbs
<h2 id="title">Welcome to Ember</h2>

{{outlet}}


{{val-example2}}
```

This will display the second component example in our application template.

12. Start the Ember server and enter invalid values for age and e-mail, and click on the **Check** button. The following image will be displayed:

After clicking on the **Check** button, an action is triggered. The validators we created earlier check the text and return whether the text is valid or not. In this instance, the text is not valid so it displays an error message.

How it works...

Data form validation is an extremely important feature of any web app. Any Ember application that has any type of user forms will need to validate data. Ember.js can retrieve data from templates and validate it. Other properties can be used to toggle or set error messages to be displayed.

The Ember CP validations add-on makes this process easier. You can create your own validations or use some of the built-in ones. This code uses computed properties and other methods to validate and report back issues to the user.

There are several other popular validation add-ons available on Ember. Check out this website for more information: `http://emberobserver.com/categories/validations`

Using D3.js with Ember.js

D3.js is a JavaScript library used to manipulate document data. It can be used to create shapes, animations, and powerful visualizations. It uses web standards such as HTML, SVG, and CSS to accomplish its goals.

Ember.js can use D3 by importing it as a library using Bower or using it as an add-on. We'll be trying it out using Bower. However, you can install the popular `ember-cli-d3` package (`ember install ember-cli-d3`) instead and get some extra functionality.

How to do it...

1. In a new application, run these commands in the `application` folder:

```
$ bower install d3 -save
$ ember g component d3-code
```

The `bower` command will install D3 and save it to the `bower.json` file. The component will end up holding all our D3 code.

2. Edit the `ember-cli-build.js` file and add the `d3` file:

```
// ember-cli-build.js
/*jshint node:true*/
/* global require, module */
var EmberApp = require('ember-cli/lib/broccoli/ember-app');

module.exports = function(defaults) {
    var app = new EmberApp(defaults, {
        // Add options here
});

app.import('bower_components/d3/d3.js');
return app.toTree();
};
```

This file is where we can add all our third-party libraries. To add D3, we have to add the `app.import` statement pointing to the directory where the D3 library is. At this point, D3 will be available to use anywhere in the application.

3. Open the `d3-code.js` template file and add a `div` tag:

```
<div id='holder'></div>
```

This will be our placeholder for the animation we'll be creating later.

4. Edit the `d3-code.js` file in the `components` folder. Add a new circle animation:

```
// app/components/d3-code.js
import Ember from 'ember';

export default Ember.Component.extend({
    didInsertElement() {
```

```
let svgContainer = d3.select('#holder')
  .append('svg').attr('width',700)
.attr('height',700);


svgContainer.append('circle').attr('cx',250)
.attr('cy',250)
.attr('r', 100)
.transition()
.attr('cx',500)
.attr('cy',450)
.duration(2000)
.style('fill','red');


  }
});
```

This component's purpose is to use D3 to create a new svg tag and a new circle object in it. To accomplish this, we want to render it on screen after the component loads. Ember.js views (components) have didInsertElement, willInsertElement, and willDestroyElement hooks. These all correspond to different points in the component's application life cycle.

The willInsertElement hook takes place after the view has rendered but before it has been inserted into the DOM. The didInsertElement hook occurs after the view has been inserted into the DOM. It's the most useful hook to use when dealing with third-party libraries such as D3. The willDestroyElement hook is called before the element is removed from the DOM. This is a good place to put code that removes event handlers that you might have added.

The svgContainer variable creates the svg tag and appends it to the div holder we created earlier. The circle variable appends the circle tag that will be animated.

5. Add the component to the application template:

    ```
    // app/templates/application.hbs
    ```

    ```
    {{d3-code}}
    ```

    This adds the component to the application template so that it can be rendered.

6. Run `ember server` and you'll see the circle move from one side of the screen to the other:

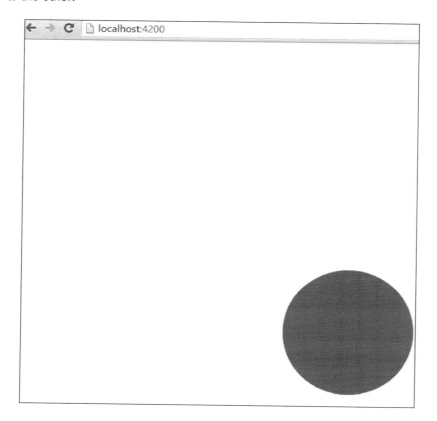

The circle will move from the top left-hand side corner to the bottom right-hand side corner after the page loads. This occurs after the component is completely rendered on screen.

How it works...

D3 uses web standards to generate powerful visualizations. Ember can import any third-party library using the built-in Broccoli library. Once a library is loaded, it can be accessed throughout the application. We can use the `didInsertElement` hook in our view to manipulate the DOM. D3 will render a circle on the screen and animate it.

Using Ember with Sockets

WebSockets make it possible to open a communication session with a server. Ember.js does not handle this natively. However, there are some easy-to-use add-ons that can be used to make this possible.

How to do it...

1. In a new application, generate a new route and install the WebSockets add-on:

   ```
   $ ember install ember-websockets
   $ ember g component w-s
   $ ember g route ws
   ```

   This will install the component route and add-on that we need to begin.

2. In the `components` template folder, edit the `w-s.hbs` file:

   ```
   // app/templates/components/w-s.hbs
   Welcome Chat!<br><br>

   Received Message: {{message}}<br>
   <button id="sendButtonPressed" {{action
     "sendButtonPressed"}}>Press Me</button>
   ```

   In this template, we have a `message` property and button that sends an action, `sendButtonPressed`. When the action is triggered, a message is sent to the server. The `message` property will display any messages returned from the server.

3. Update the `w-s.js` component file so that it can handle the action from the template:

   ```
   // app/components/w-s.js
   import Ember from 'ember';

   export default Ember.Component.extend({
       websockets: Ember.inject.service(),
       socket: null,
       init() {
         this._super();
         let socket = this.get('websockets')
           .socketFor('ws://localhost:7000/');
         this.set('socket',socket);
         socket.on('open', this.myOpenHandler, this);
         socket.on('message', this.myMessageHandler, this);
   ```

```
        socket.on('close', (event)=> {
          console.log('closed');
        }, this);
      },
      message: '',

      myOpenHandler(event) {
        console.log('On open event has been called: ' +
          event);
      },

      myMessageHandler(event) {
        console.log('Message: ' + event.data);
        this.set('message',event.data);
      },

      actions: {
        sendButtonPressed() {
          this.get('socket').send('Hello Websocket World');
        }
      }
    });
```

The add-on installs a service called `websockets` in the application. It can be accessed by injecting it into the component using `Ember.inject.service`. As the property name matches the service name, we don't need to specify the service name in the inject statement.

4. To begin, we'll set up the `init` function:

    ...

    ```
    init() {
      this._super();
      let socket = this.get('websockets')
        .socketFor('ws://localhost:7000/');
      this.set('socket',socket);
      socket.on('open', this.myOpenHandler, this);
      socket.on('message', this.myMessageHandler, this);
      socket.on('close', (event)=> {
        console.log('closed');
      },this);
    },
    ```

    ...

The `init` function in a component is called on when the object is instantiated. You can override this by setting up your own `init`. To make sure that nothing odd occurs, we must call `this._super()` so that Ember sets up the component correctly.

The `socket.on` method creates three events called `open`, `message`, and `close`. During instantiation, these three event handlers are created. The first one handles events that occur when a connection is made with the server.

The WebSocket service can be set up using the `socketFor` method. This tells the service where the server is located.

```
...
    message: '',

    myOpenHandler(event) {
      console.log('On open event has been called: ' +
        event);
    },
...
```

When the connection is established, a message is logged to the console.

5. The second event is triggered when a message is received from the server:

```
...
    myMessageHandler(event) {
      console.log('Message: ' + event.data);
      this.set('message',event.data);
    },
...
```

6. After a message is received, it's set to the `message` property. The last event is triggered when the connection with the server is closed:

```
...
    socket.on('close', (event)=> {
      console.log('closed');
    }, this);
..
```

This logs a message to the console.

7. The `sendButtonPressed` action creates a message and sends it to the server:

```
...
    actions: {
      sendButtonPressed() {
        this.get('socket').send('Hello Websocket World');
      }
    }
...
```

After the action is triggered, we use the existing `socket` property to send a message out to the server.

8. Add the `w-s` component to the `ws.hbs` route:

```
// app/templates/ws.hbs
{{w-s}}
```

The component will render at `{{w-s}}`.

9. Load the server and navigate to the `w-s` route at `/ws`. You'll see the following message:

This message displays the values from the server. Pressing the button sends a message to the server.

You can see how we can take this simple example and create a complete chat server.

How it works...

WebSockets helps facilitate communication between a server and browser. The browser can send and receive data over sockets. This can be used with event-driven messages or APIs.

There's more...

There are many ways to implement a WebSockets server. A great way to do this is to use the ws library. In the following steps, we'll create a basic WebSockets server to use with this recipe:

1. Create a new empty directory and run this command:

```
$ npm init
```

Follow the prompts and create your project.

2. Install the ws package:

```
$ npm install ws -save
```

This will install the ws npm package and save it to the package.json file.

3. Create a new server.js file. Create a simple WebSockets server:

```
// server.js
var WebSocketServer = require('ws').Server;
var ws = new WebSocketServer({port: 7000});


ws.on('connection', function connection(ws) {
ws.on('message', function incoming(message) {
    console.log('received: %s', message);
    ws.send('Hey! Welcome to my websocket challenge!');
});


});
```

4. Start the node server:

```
$ node ./server.js
```

This server creates port open at 7000. It then waits for a connection. If it receives a message, it outputs it to the console and returns a new message. This will be displayed in the Ember template file and received by the message handler.

Using Ember with Firebase

Firebase is a backend as a service provider. It can store data and authenticate your users with just a few lines of code. It integrates well with many different frameworks, including Ember.js.

In this recipe, we'll take a look at a few of the features of Firebase by creating a blogging application. This app will allow users to create, edit, or delete posts. Users will be able to log in with Twitter and be authenticated as well.

Getting ready

Before getting started, we must set up an account with Firebase at http://www.firebase. com. Google owns Firebase so this should be really easy. In fact, you should be able to log in directly with your Google credentials.

After logging in, you'll need to create a new application and set up a new provider. Follow these steps:

1. Create a new application in the Firebase dashboard. It should look like the following image. Write down **APP URL** for later:

2. After creating the app, click on **manage** and then click on the left-hand side, where it says **Login & Auth**. Click on **Twitter** and enter your **Twitter API Key** and **Twitter API Secret**:

To get these keys, you'll need to create a new application through Twitter. To do this, go to `apps.twitter.com` and click on **CREATE NEW APP**. Follow the onscreen instructions. Make sure to set the callback URL to `https://auth.firebase.com/auth/twitter/callback`.

This should be it. Make sure that you write down the name of the URL that Firebase created. You'll need it later when you set everything up in the `environment.js` file.

How to do it...

1. In a new application, generate and install these files:

   ```
   $ ember install emberfire
   $ ember install torii
   $ ember install ember-bootstrap
   $ ember install ember-cli-showdown
   $ ember g route new
   $ ember g route posts
   $ ember g route application
   $ ember g controller new
   $ ember g controller posts
   $ ember g model post title:string body:string author:string
   titleURL:string
   $ ember g template index
   $ ember g util clean
   ```

   The files generated will be the skeleton of our application. The two `install` commands will install the necessary files for Firebase with authentication using an add-on called `torii`.

2. Verify that the application adapter is set up for Firebase:

   ```
   // app/adapters/application.js
   import Ember from 'ember';
   import FirebaseAdapter from 'emberfire/adapters/firebase';

   const { inject } = Ember;

   export default FirebaseAdapter.extend({
     firebase: inject.service(),
   });
   ```

   This adapter is automatically generated for us when we install the `emberfire` add-on. It injects the Firebase service into our application and data store.

3. Configure the `emberfire` adapter by editing the `environment.js` file:

```
// config/environment.js
...
    firebase: 'https://testemberfire.firebaseio.com/',
    torii: {
      sessionServiceName: 'session'
    },
...
```

To use Firebase, you must set the `firebase` property to your Firebase URL that you created earlier. Make sure that the `torii` property is also set so that we can use the `session` object in our application.

4. Add a new folder called `torii-adapters` and add the `application.js` file:

```
// app/tori-adapters/application.js
import Ember from 'ember';
import ToriiFirebaseAdapter from 'emberfire/torii-adapters/
firebase';
export default ToriiFirebaseAdapter.extend({
    firebase: Ember.inject.service()
});
```

Torii is a type of authentication abstraction for Ember.js. This will make it possible to use the session variable in our program.

5. Update the `clean.js` file in the `utils` folder:

```
// app/utils/clean.js
export default function clean(title) {
    title = title.replace(/ /g, '_');
    return title.replace(/[^a-zA-Z0-9-_]/g, '');
}
```

This file is simply used to clean a URL and return it. In other words, it removes anything other than dashes and the characters, `a-z`. We'll be using this later for our URLs.

6. Let's take a look at the model file and make sure that it looks *OK*:

```
// app/models/post.js
import DS from 'ember-data';

export default DS.Model.extend({
    title: DS.attr('string'),
    body: DS.attr('string'),
    author: DS.attr('string'),
```

```
    titleURL: DS.attr('string')

});
```

The model contains all the data we'll be using for each post in our application. This should have been generated earlier.

7. Update the `router.js` file using the `titleURL` as the path:

```
// app/router.js
import Ember from 'ember';
import config from './config/environment';

const Router = Ember.Router.extend({
    location: config.locationType
});

Router.map(function() {
    this.route('posts', {path: '/:titleURL'}, function() {
});
    this.route('new');
});

export default Router;
```

Some of this was generated for us when we created the posts and new route. However, we want to make sure that `titleURL` is set to the path of each individual post. We do this by passing the `:titleURL` dynamic segment to the path.

8. Add the query for each individual post to the posts route:

```
// app/routes/posts.js
import Ember from 'ember';

export default Ember.Route.extend({
    model(param) {
      return this.store.query('post', {
        orderBy: 'titleURL',
        equalTo: param.titleURL });
    }
});
```

When the user navigates to the `/posts` URL, the model will expect a parameter passed in. For example, if you navigate to `/posts/my_post`, the `my_post` segment will be passed as a parameter that can be accessed in the route. We'll use this parameter in the Firebase `this.store.query` method. The first argument is the name of the model. We can then use `orderBy` and `equalTo` to specify the exact post that we are looking for.

Uniqueness

As you can imagine, when creating a new post, the title may or may not be unique. The `this.store.query` method will return all results as an array to the model. We could enforce uniqueness in Firebase by making the `titleURL` unique. Another possibility would be to check the uniqueness of the post title during creation. Either way, for this example, we'll assume that all titleURLs are unique.

9. Edit the application route file and add the model and a few actions:

```
// app/routes/application.js
import Ember from 'ember';

export default Ember.Route.extend({
    model(){
        return this.store.findAll('post');
    },
    actions:{
        login(){
            this.get('session').open('firebase', { provider:
                'twitter'}).then((data)=> {
            });
        },
        logout(){
            this.get('session').close();
        }
    }
});
```

We want the main application to have access to the model route so that we can use the `findAll` method to retrieve all posts. This is basically the same as the Ember Data method we've used in previous recipes.

There are two actions, `login` and `logout`. As we injected, using `torii`, our session into the program, we can access it from anywhere. By invoking `this.get('session')`, we can open or close a session. Firebase has several built-in authenticators, including Twitter and Facebook. The `login` action in this example will open a window to `twitter` so that the user can be authenticated.

Firebase security

With any JavaScript browser application, security can be tricky. Firebase makes this a little easier for us. Firebase keeps track of users that are authenticated. In the Firebase dashboard, you can set rules that make it possible for only authenticated users to receive data. This is a little beyond the scope of this recipe. However, it is possible to secure your data with Firebase using a third-party authenticator such as Twitter or Facebook.

10. Open the application template file. Add a navigation bar at the top and buttons to log in, log out, and add a new post:

```
//app/templates/application.hbs
<nav class="navbar navbar-inverse navbar-fixed-top">
    <div class="container-fluid">
    <div class="navbar-header" href="#">
    {{#link-to 'index' class='navbar-brand'}}My New
      Blog{{/link-to}}
    </div>
    <ul class="nav navbar-nav">
    {{#if session.isAuthenticated}}
    <li>{{#link-to 'new'}}Add New Post{{/link-to}}</li>
    {{/if}}
    </ul>
    <ul class="nav navbar-nav navbar-right">
    {{#unless session.isAuthenticated}}
    <li><a href="#" {{action 'login' }}>Login</a></li>
    {{else}}
    <li><a href="#" {{action 'logout' }}>Logout</a></li>
    {{/unless}}
    </ul>
    </div>
</nav>
<br>
<br>
<br>
{{outlet}}
```

As we have installed the `ember-bootstrap` add-on, we can create a really simple top navigation bar. The `login` and `logout` buttons are surrounded by the `if` helper. In every template, you have access to the `session` property. This property has a method called `isAuthenticated` that returns `true` if the user is logged in and `false` if the user is not logged in. We can use this to show the `login` button only if the user is *NOT* logged in. If the user is logged in, they'll see a `logout` button.

We don't have an application controller, so these actions will bubble up to the application route where they'll be handled.

11. Now update the `index.hbs` file with a link to each individual post:

```
// app/templates/index.hbs

<div class = 'row'>
    <div class='col-md-4'>
      <h1>Posts</h1>
        {{#each model as |post|}}
          <br>{{#link-to 'posts'
            post.titleURL}}{{post.title}}{{/link-to}}
        {{/each}}
    </div>

</div>
```

The `model` loops through each post and displays the `title` on the screen. Each `titleURL` is passed as a parameter to the posts route.

12. In the new template, add some textboxes so that the user can add a post. Add a section to preview a post as well:

```
// app/templates/new.hbs
<br><br>
<div class='col-md-4 border' >
    <h1>New Post</h1>
    <form {{action 'save' on="submit"}}>
      <dl>
        <dt>Title:<br> {{textarea value=title cols="40" |
          rows="1" placeholder='Title'}}</dt>
        <dt>Body:<br> {{textarea value=body cols="40"
          rows="6" placeholder='Body'}}</dt>
      </dl>
      <button type='submit' class='btn btn-
        primary'>Add</button>
    </form>
</div>
<div class='col-md-4 border'  >
    <h1>Preview</h1>
    <h3>{{title}}</h3>
    <h4>{{markdown-to-html markdown=body}}</h4>
</div>
```

The new template will be used to create a new post. The `textarea` helper creates two textboxes. The form has a `save` action that will be triggered when the form is submitted.

When setting up the project, we installed a `markdown` add-on. This allows us to use `markdown` in the body of the post. Markdown is a text-to-HTML conversion tool. It makes it easier to write HTML in your text.

13. In the posts template, display each post and show a way to edit the post as well:

```
// app/templates/posts.js
{{#each model as |model|}}
<div class='row'>
    {{#if isEditing}}
      <div class='col-md-4 border'>
        <form {{action 'save' on='submit'}}>
          <dl>
            <dt>Title:<br> {{textarea value=model.title
                cols='40' rows='1'}}</dt>
            <dt>Body:<br> {{textarea value=model.body
                cols='40' rows='6'}}</dt>
          </dl>
        <div class = 'row'>
          <button type='submit' class =
            'btn btn-primary'>Done</button>
        </div>
        </form>
      </div>
    {{/if}}
    <div class='col-md-4 border'>
      <h1>{{model.title}}</h1>
      <h3>{{markdown-to-html markdown=model.body}}</h3>
      <h4>-{{model.author}}</h4>
      {{#if session.isAuthenticated}}
        <form {{action 'edit' }}>
        <button type='submit' class=
          'btn btn-primary'>Edit</button>
            <button type='delete' class= 'btn btn-primary'
              {{action 'delete'}}>Delete</button>
        </form>
      {{/if}}
    </div>
</div>
{{/each}}
```

This displays each individual post. If the user is authenticated, they can either delete or edit the post.

Once again, we use the `textarea` template helpers to display the textboxes. The form has an edit action attached that will set the `isEditing` property to `true` so that the post can be edited. The `delete` action deletes the post.

14. Add the `save` action to the new controller:

```
// app/controllers/new.js
import Ember from 'ember';
import cleanURI from '../utils/clean';

export default Ember.Controller.extend({
    actions: {
      save(){

          const titleURL= cleanURI(this.get('title'));
          const post = this.store.createRecord('post',{
          title: this.get('title'),
          body: this.get('body'),
          author: 'test',
          titleURL: titleURL
          });
          post.save();
          this.set('title','');
          this.set('body','');
          this.transitionToRoute('index');
      }
    }
});
```

The `save` action is used to save the data to Firebase. First, it takes the title of the post and uses the utility, `cleanURI`, to remove all special characters and spaces. Firebase has a function called `createRecord` that is used to create new records. We then save the record to the store and `set` the values back to default. Finally, the application transitions back to the index.

15. In the posts controller, add actions for `edit`, `delete`, and `save`:

```
// app/controllers/posts.js
import Ember from 'ember';
import cleanURI from '../utils/clean';

export default Ember.Controller.extend({
    actions: {
      edit(){
        this.set('isEditing', true);
      },
```

```
      delete(){
        this.get('model').forEach(model=>{
          model.deleteRecord();
        });
        this.get('model').save();
        this.set('isEditing', false);
        this.transitionToRoute('index');
      },
      save(){
        this.get('model').forEach(model=>{
          const titleURL = cleanURI(model.get('title'));
          model.set('titleURL', titleURL);
          model.save();
        });
        this.set('isEditing',false);
        this.transitionToRoute('index');
      }
    }
});
```

Let's break this down into more detail:

...

```
    edit(){
      this.set('isEditing',true);
    },
```

...

The edit function sets the isEditing property to true. The posts template uses this property to show or not show the editing window:

...

```
    delete(){
      this.get('model').forEach(model=>{
        model.deleteRecord();
      });
      this.get('model').save();
      this.set('isEditing',false);
      this.transitionToRoute('index');
    },
```

...

The `delete` action deletes the record. To do this, we must use the `forEach` method on our `model`. In the route, we used the `query` method, which returns an array. Therefore, we have to go through every record returned, and delete it. Once again, we'll assume that every title is unique and only has one record. Remember to always `.save()` so that the record is persisted in Firebase. After the record is deleted, we transition to the index route:

```
...
save () {
  this.get('model').forEach(model=>{
    const titleURL = cleanURI(model.get('title'));
    model.set('titleURL',titleURL);
    model.save();
  });
  this.set('isEditing',false);
  this.transitionToRoute('index');
}
...
```

The `save` function gets the title, cleans it, sets it, and saves the model. In this example, we must use the `forEach` method to iterate over the array. Afterward, we set the `isEditing` property back to `false` and transition back to the `index`.

16. Run the application and the following screen will be displayed:

This displays the top left corner of the screen. No posts are listed as we haven't added them yet:

17. The top right corner of the screen will show the **Login** button. We'll need to log in by pressing this button. This will bring a popup asking for credentials to our Twitter account. After logging in, the **Add New Post** text will be displayed:

18. Clicking on **Add New Post** will display the following screen:

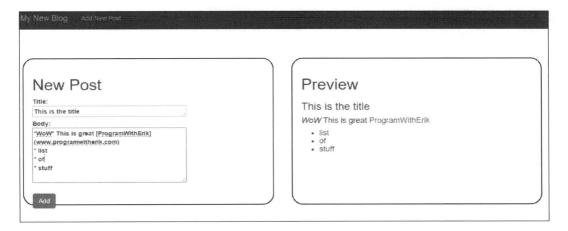

19. You can see that the preview takes the markdown and converts it to HTML. After adding the new post, it will then be listed:

20. Clicking on the title will bring us to an edit screen. Here, we can **Edit** or **Delete** the post:

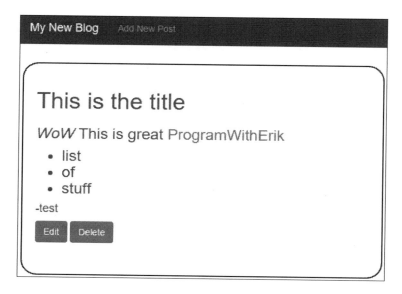

21. Clicking on the **Edit** button will bring up the edit screen:

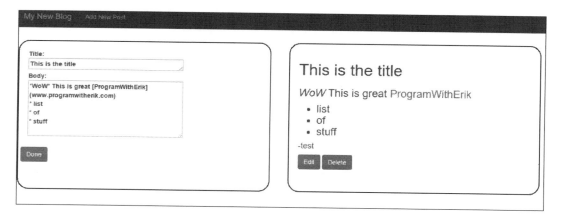

From here, we can make any changes and save it back again. Each time a save occurs, the post is persisted in Firebase.

How it works...

Firebase talks to its backend service via the `emberfire` and `torii` add-ons. EmberFire is an official Ember Data adapter. It has many of the same features as other popular adapters. It can save, delete, edit, and query data fairly easily. One of its purposes is to make it really easy to persist and save data without having to set up your own backend.

Firebase also has authentication providers that it can hook into. Firebase handles all the authentication between the provider and application. All that this requires is that the provider is set up in Firebase.

Using server side rendering

Ember.js runs in the browser. It uses JavaScript to handle all the routing and rendering of data. It only talks to the server on the initial page load and to retrieve JSON data. This can have some limitations. Larger applications might take longer to load on slower connections and there is still some concern around search engine optimization.

To help alleviate these concerns, the Ember team created **FastBoot**. FastBoot is an Ember CLI add-on that allows Ember.js to render and serve applications on the server. It's a work in progress as of writing this and has some limitations. It's not recommended for production and doesn't work with jQuery or `didInsertElement`. It will hopefully be production-ready by Ember v2.4.

Nevertheless, it's improving and is an important add-on for Ember.

How to do it...

1. In a new application, run these commands:

   ```
   $ ember install ember-cli-fastboot
   $ rm -rf bower_components
   $ bower install --save ember#canary
   ```

   FastBoot requires the `canary` version of Ember to work. We must delete the `bower_components` folder before installing. During installation, you may get a message that Bower cannot find a suitable version of Ember. This is normal; make sure to choose `ember#canary` from the list.

2. Build the application for production:

   ```
   $ ember build -prod
   ```

   This will build the production server and minify all the files.

3. Run the Ember FastBoot server:

    ```
    $ ember fastboot --serve-assets --port 4200 --environment
    production
    ```

    This will run the FastBoot server. Let's break down these arguments:

    - **--serve-assets**: This serves the assets out of the `dist` folder.
    - **--port 4200**: This specifies the port. The default is 3000. In this case, we can use `4200` to match the test server that we normally use.
    - **--environment production**: The default is development. Use production. It works better as Ember FastBoot is faster with minified files.

4. Open up localhost at port `4200` to see the web page load:

The page doesn't look any different. However, if you look at the browser console, you'll notice that the Ember application rendered without downloading all the JavaScript it normally needs to run in the browser.

How it works...

Ember FastBoot is an Ember add-on that's being worked on. As of writing this, it has a lot of limitations. With this said, it will eventually allow you to render your Ember.js application on the server, or at least part of the application, for the initial page load. This will help reduce page load times significantly. To learn more about Ember FastBoot, check out their website at `https://github.com/tildeio/ember-cli-fastboot`.

11
Real-Time Web Applications

In this chapter, we'll cover the following recipes:

- ▶ Using dependency injection
- ▶ Working with application initializers
- ▶ Building a chat application
- ▶ Creating and working with add-ons
- ▶ Learning the Ember run loop

Introduction

As you level up with Ember, you'll learn how to work with real-time applications. In these types of applications, you'll be dealing with updates from a server. You'll need to be able to handle these events and notify the user as needed.

In Ember, we can use things such as dependency injection and services with WebSockets to handle real-time events from a server. We'll be looking at these concepts, including add-ons, in this chapter.

Using dependency injection

The dependency injection pattern is used to declare and instantiate classes of objects and handle dependencies between them. In Ember, we can take objects or services and inject them into routes, controllers, or components.

In this recipe, we'll take a logger object and inject it into our controllers using dependency injection.

How to do it...

1. In a new application, install the `moment` library and create a new `initializer`:

    ```
    $ bower install moment -save
    $ ember g initializer application
    ```

    This will install the Bower **Moment.js** library. We'll use this for our custom logger.

2. Import the Moment library to the Ember project:

    ```
    // ember-cli-build.js
    /*jshint node:true*/
    /* global require, module */
    var EmberApp = require('ember-cli/lib/broccoli/ember-app');

    module.exports = function(defaults) {
        var app = new EmberApp(defaults, {
          // Add options here
        });

        app.import
          ('bower_components/moment/min/moment.min.js');
          return app.toTree();
    };
    ```

    The `app.import` statement adds the `moment` library to the application.

3. In the `application.js` file in the `initializers` folder, add a new logger:

    ```
    // app/initializers/application.js
    /* global moment */
    import Ember from 'ember';

    export function initialize( application) {
        let MyLogger = Ember.Object.extend({
          log(info){
            let time = moment().format();
    ```

```
        Ember.Logger.debug(`(${time}):`,info);
      }
    });
    application.register('myLogger:zzz', MyLogger);
    application.inject
      ('controller','myLogger','myLogger:zzz');
}

export default {
    name: 'application',
    initialize
};
```

This creates a new logger called `myLogger`. It uses the built-in `Ember.Logger` and adds a timestamp to it using the `moment` library that was installed earlier.

Let's take a look at this in more detail:

```
    application.register('myLogger:zzz', MyLogger);
```

The `application.register` method registers a new factory. The first argument is the registration key. The registration key is always two parts separated by a colon `:`. The first part is the type of factory and the second part is the name of the factory. The type of factory can be a template, `component`, `controller`, or `service`, or you can create your own. In this example, I called it `myLogger`. The second argument is the object you want to register, `MyLogger`:

```
    application.inject
      ('controller','myLogger','myLogger:zzz');
```

This application inject makes the new `myLogger:zzz` factory available in all controllers. The value of `myLogger` comes from the `myLogger:zzz` factory.

4. Create a new application controller and add a new action that logs using the new `myLogger` debugger:

```
// app/controllers/application.js
import Ember from 'ember';

export default Ember.Controller.extend({
    actions: {
      press(){
        this.myLogger.log('Hello World!');


      }
    });
```

When a new `press` action occurs, it logs to the console, `Hello World`.

5. Add `action` to the application template:

    ```
    <h2 id="title">Welcome to Ember</h2>

    {{outlet}}
    <button {{action 'press'}}>Button</button>
    ```

    When the button is clicked, the `press` action is triggered.

6. Run `ember server` and you'll see the following screen:

    Press **Button** and you'll see something as follows in the console:

    ```
    DEBUG: ------------------------------------
    DEBUG: Ember        : 2.2.0
    DEBUG: Ember Data   : 2.2.1
    DEBUG: jQuery       : 1.11.3
    DEBUG: ------------------------------
    (2015-12-26T17:06:40-08:00): Hello World!
    (2015-12-26T17:06:41-08:00): Hello World!
    |
    ```

    Each time you click the button, it logs a debug statement to the console.

How it works...

Dependency injection occurs when we take objects and inject them into other objects during instantiation. Ember can do this with the `application.inject` method. To accomplish this in Ember, we must create factories. Factories are simply objects that return other objects.

Ember registers these factories in `Ember.Application`. `Ember.Application` acts as a registry of sorts that holds different factories. After being registered, they can be injected into other parts of the Ember application such as components or controllers.

Working with application initializers

Application initializers can be used to configure your application as it boots. It's the primary place to set up dependency injections in your application.

In this example, we'll examine when an application initializer is run.

How to do it...

1. In a new application, create `initializer`:

   ```
   $ ember g initializer application
   ```

   This will create a new application `initializer`. This will be run as soon as the application boots.

2. Add an alert box to the initializer:

   ```
   // app/initializers/application.js
   export function initialize( application ) {
       alert('loading application');
   }

   export default {
       name: 'application',
       initialize
   };
   ```

   This will load an `alert` box as soon as the application loads.

3. Run `ember server` and you should see an alert box displayed before the application is loaded:

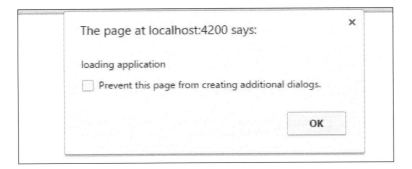

   Nothing else has loaded in the application before this alert box is shown.

4. If needed, we can also `register` or `inject` services in the initializer. It may look as follows:

```
// app/initializer/application.js
export function initialize(app) {
    app.inject('component', 'start', 'service:start');
}

export default {
    name: 'init',
    initialize
};
```

This takes the service named start and injects it into all the components. You can see more examples of this in *Chapter 9, Real-Life Tasks with Ember.js*.

Application instance initializers

Application instance initializers run when the instance is loaded. It was added with Ember's FastBoot to make it easier to run many requests concurrently. During bootup, application initializers are run first, then instance initializers. If needed, you can look up factories you've already registered in the application initializer in the instance initializer.

For the most part, you'll only be using instance initializers for certain A/B testing configurations, configuring initial states, and when working with the Ember FastBoot server. To generate an instance initializer, run `ember g instance-initializer <name>`.

How it works...

Application initializers are run as soon as the application boots. This is the primary place to configure dependency injections into your application. Try to keep initializers as lightweight as possible. More complexity added to an initializer might cause delay in the application loading. Things like asynchronous loading conditions will work better in a service or route hook instead.

Building a chat application

In this recipe, we'll combine what you learned with initializers and dependency injection to create a chat room. The chat room will use WebSockets to communicate with the host.

How to do it...

1. In a new application, generate these files:

   ```
   $ ember g service sockjs
   $ ember g component chat-room
   $ ember g initializer application
   $ bower install sockjs --save
   ```

   These will generate the files needed for the project. The `chat-room` component will have all the logic for the chat room that we'll create.

2. Import the **SockJS** library to the application:

   ```
   // ember-cli-build.js
   ...
   app.import('bower_components/sockjs/sockjs.min.js');
   ...
   ```

   This will import the library so that we can use the global variable, `sockjs`, anywhere in our application.

3. Create a new service for `SockJS`:

   ```
   // app/services/sockjs.js
   /* global SockJS */
   import Ember from 'ember';
   const {run} = Ember;

   export default Ember.Service.extend(Ember.Evented, {
       socket: null,
       init() {
         this._super();
         let socket = new SockJS('http://localhost:7000');
         socket.addEventListener('message',
           run.bind(this, (event)=> {
           this.trigger('messageReceived', event.data);
           console.log(event.data);
         }));
         this.set('socket',socket);
       },
       sendInfo(message) {
         this.get('socket').send(message);

       }

   });
   ```

Let's take a look at this in more detail:

```
/* global SockJS */
```

This line is needed so that **JSHint** won't complain about the SockJS global variable. JSHint is the built-in library for Ember CLI that detects errors in your program:

```
export default Ember.Service.extend(Ember.Evented,{
```

This adds the `Ember.Evented` mixin to the service. This mixin allows Ember objects to subscribe and emit events. This is perfect for what we need to do in this example:

```
init() {
    this._super(...arguments);
},
```

The `init` method is where the SockJS socket will be set up and the event listener will be created. This method will fire after the service is initialized. The `this._super` method guarantees that the `init` method is set up properly:

```
let socket = new SockJS('http://localhost:7000');
```

The preceding line creates a new socket server at the localhost port `7000`:

```
socket.addEventListener
    ('message', run.bind(this, (event)=> {
    this.trigger('messageReceived', event.data);
    console.log(event.data);
})));
this.set('socket',socket);
```

This creates an event listener that is fired when a message is received. The `run.bind` method is a part of the Ember `run` loop that we'll describe later in this chapter. This ensures that all the requests are taken care of properly in the `run` loop.

The `this.trigger` is a part of the `Event.Evented` class. The `trigger` method creates a new event called `messageReceived`. We can subscribe to this event so that other methods in Ember can be triggered when a message is received. Finally, we `log` the information in `event.data` to the console and `set` the `socket` property:

```
sendInfo(message) {
    this.get('socket').send(message);
}
```

This method accepts `message` and sends it the `socket` server we defined earlier. The `socket` property is accessed here.

4. Inject the new service into all the components in the application:

```
// app/initializers/application.js
export function initialize( application ) {
    application.inject('component', 'sockjs', 'service:sockjs');
}

export default {
    name: 'websockets',
    initialize
};
```

The initializer takes the service called `sockjs` and injects it into all the components. This will be run whenever the program first boots. We use this so that we don't have to specifically inject the `sockjs` service into each component.

5. Create a new component for the chat room:

```
// app/components/chat-room.js
import Ember from 'ember';
const {$} = Ember;


export default Ember.Component.extend({
    message: '',

    init() {
      this._super(...arguments);
      this.sockjs.on('messageReceived',this,
        'messageReceived');
    },

    messageReceived(message){
      $('#chat-content').val((i, text) =>
      `${text}${message}\n`;
      );
      this.set('message',message);
    },
    actions: {
      enter(info,username) {
        this.sockjs.sendInfo(`${username}: ${info}`);

      }
    }

});
```

Let's break this down into smaller parts:

```
init() {
  this._super(…arguments);
  this.sockjs.on('messageReceived',this,
    'messageReceived');
},
```

This `init` method fires on initialization and sets up the component. We can then subscribe to the event that we created earlier in the service using on. The first parameter is the name of the event. The second is the binding. The last is the name of the callback function. Therefore, in this example, whenever a message is received in the service, the `messageReceived` callback in this component will be fired:

```
messageReceived(message){
  $('#chat-content').val((i, text)=>
  `${text}${message}\n`
  );
  this.set('message',message);
```

This is the `messageReceived` callback. It uses a little bit of jQuery to find the `chat-content` ID and concatenate the existing message to it using ES6 string interpolation. In addition, the `message` property is set:

```
actions: {
  enter(info,username) {
    this.sockjs.sendInfo(`${username}: ${info}`);

  }
}
```

This action sends `info` and `username` to the socket. This way, any other clients connected will be notified.

6. Create the `chat-room.hbs` template file for the component:

```
// app/templates/components/chat-room.hbs

<textarea id="chat-content"
  style="width:500px;height:300px" ></textarea><br/>
{{input type='text' placeholder='User Name'
  value=uname}}
{{input type='text' placeholder='Chat Message'
  value=mess}}
<button {{action 'enter' mess uname}}>Send</button><br>

Message received:{{message}}
```

This code displays the messages from the server. The `input` helpers capture the username and message. Each value is passed to the `enter` action when the `Send` button is clicked.

7. Add the component to the `application.hbs` file:

```
// app/templates/application.hbs
<h2 id="title">Welcome to Ember</h2>

{{outlet}}
{{chat-room}}
```

This adds the component to the application.

8. Start the node server. Then start the Ember application. You'll see the following screen:

As each client connects they'll be able to send messages to the server. Each client will receive these messages and display them in the chat box.

How it works...

A chat room consists of multiple clients talking to a server. The server's job is to notify all the other clients connected when a messages is received. This is done in this example using SockJS with WebSockets. The SockJS library has message events that we can set up in Ember. When a message is received, it is then sent to a component that updates its template with the message.

There's more...

To use the preceding example, you'll need to set up a WebSocket server. Here are the steps to create a simple Node.js SockJS server. To learn more about SockJS, check out their GitHub page at `https://github.com/sockjs/sockjs-node`.

1. In a new directory, run the `npm init` command:

   ```
   $ npm init
   $ npm install sockjs -save
   ```

   This will generate the `package.json` file and install the SockJS server in it.

2. Create a new `app.js` file for the WebSocket server:

   ```
   // app.js
   var http = require('http');
   var sockjs = require('sockjs');


   var clients = {};

   function broadcast(message){
       for (var client in clients){
         clients[client].write(message);
       }
   }

   var socketServer = sockjs.createServer({ sockjs_url:
     'http://cdn.jsdelivr.net/sockjs/1.0.1/sockjs.min.js' });
   socketServer.on('connection', (conn)=> {
       clients[conn.id] = conn;

       conn.on('data', (message)=> {
         console.log('received ' + message);
         broadcast(message);
       });
   ```

```
    conn.write("hello from the server thanks for
      connecting!");
    conn.on('close', ()=> {
      delete clients[conn.id];
    });
    console.log("connected");
});

var server = http.createServer();
socketServer.installHandlers(server);
server.listen(7000, '0.0.0.0');
```

This server uses the SockJS library to create a new socket server. When a new client connects, it's added to an array. When it receives data, it broadcasts this data to all the other servers connected using this function:

```
function broadcast(message){
    for (var client in clients){
      clients[client].write(message);
    }
}
```

This function sends a `broadcast message` to every other client connected with the `message` it just received. When Ember receives this information, it's written to the chat box.

Creating and working with add-ons

Ember has a common way of sharing code using something called Ember Addons (also known as add-ons). Ember Addons make it easy to distribute reusable libraries with other applications. Anyone can create add-ons. You can publish them to NPM or to your own private Git repository.

Keep in mind that you can also use Bower to install frontend dependencies. This is done through the Bower package manager. Take a look at *Chapter 1, Ember CLI Basics* for more information on how to do this.

In this recipe, we'll take our chat program from the last section and make it an add-on.

How to do it...

1. Create a new add-on called `sockjs-chat`. Generate these files:

```
$ ember addon sockjs-chat
$ cd sockjs-chat
$ ember g component sockjs-chat
$ ember g service sockjs
$ ember g blueprint sockjs-chat
$ npm install ember-cli-htmlbars --save
```

The `ember addon` command generates the folder structure for the add-on. We'll discuss the folder structure in more detail later. The `blueprint` command creates a new blueprint called `sockjs-chat`. Blueprints are used to generate snippets of code. This is needed so that the SockJS library can be installed. If we're doing anything with templates, we'll need to add `ember-cli-htmlbars`.

2. Create the `sockjs-chat` blueprint so that it installs the SockJS library:

```
// blueprints/sockjs-chat/index.js
/*jshint node:true*/
module.exports = {
    normalizeEntityName() {
},

    afterInstall() {
      return this.addBowerPackageToProject('sockjs-client',
        '~1.0.3');
    }
};
```

The `afterInstall` hook is used to add Bower packages. By default, the blueprint file will be run during the add-on installation. This guarantees that the `sockjs-client` library is installed via the Bower package manager.

3. Update the root `index.js` file so that the SockJS library is imported:

```
// index.js
/* jshint node: true */
'use strict';

module.exports = {
    name: 'sockjs-chat',
      included(app) {
        this._super.included(app);
```

```
    app.import(app.bowerDirectory +
        '/sockjs-client/dist/sockjs.min.js');
    }
};
```

The JavaScript SockJS library is installed in the blueprint. However, we still need to import it to Ember. This can be done in the root folder's `index.js` file. This file is the entry point to the application. The `included` hook is used to import the Bower components to the application. Imports are added to the application in the order that they appear.

4. Set the `package.json` file with the correct information for the project:

```
// package.json
{
    "name": "sockjs-chat",
    "version": "1.0.0",
    "description": "EmberJS Sockjs Chat Addon",
...
"repository": "https://github.com/ErikCH/sockjs-chat",
...
"author": "Erik Hanchett",
...
    "keywords": [
      "ember-addon",
      "sockjs",
      "ember websockets"
...
```

It's important to have your `package.json` file updated with at least your `name`, `description`, `repository`, `author`, and `keywords`. This is extremely important if you plan on open sourcing your add-on and publishing it to NPM. Without this information, your add-on will be hard to find.

5. In the generated service file, add a new `setup` and `send` method:

```
// addon/services/sockjs.js
/* global SockJS */
import Ember from 'ember';
var {run} = Ember;

export default Ember.Service.extend(Ember.Evented,{
    socket: null,
    setupSockjs(url) {
      let socket = new SockJS(url);
      socket.addEventListener('message',
        run.bind(this, (event)=> {
```

```
        this.trigger('messageReceived', event.data);
        console.log(event.data);
      }));
      this.set('socket',socket);
    },
    sendInfo(message) {
      let socket= this.get('socket');
      if(socket != null){
        socket.send(message);
      }
    }

});
```

This may look familiar. This is almost the same service that we created in the last recipe. However, this time, we have a new `setupSockjs` method that takes `url` as a parameter. The `url` parameter is used to set the new socket listener:

```
socket.addEventListener('message',
  run.bind(this, (event)=> {
  this.trigger('messageReceived', event.data);
  console.log(event.data);
  }));
```

This `event` is triggered when a new `message` is received. After a new `message` arrives, a new trigger called `messageReceived` will be called:

```
sendInfo(message) {
  let socket= this.get('socket');
  if(socket != null){
    socket.send(message);
  }
```

As long as `socket` isn't `null`, `message` will be sent to the WebSocket server.

6. Set up the `sockjs-chat.js` component:

```
// addon/components/sockjs-chat.js
import Ember from 'ember';
import layout from '../templates/components/sockjs-chat';
const {typeOf} = Ember;
export default Ember.Component.extend({

    sockjs: Ember.inject.service('sockjs'),
    layout,
    message:'',
```

```
init() {
  this._super(...arguments);
  this.get('sockjs').setupSockjs(this.attrs.url);
  this.get('sockjs').on
    ('messageReceived',this,(message)=>{
    this.set('message',message);
    this._actionHandler('receiveAction',message);
  });
},
_actionHandler(actionName, ...args) {

  if(this.attrs && typeOf(this.attrs[actionName]) ===
    'function'){
    this.attrs[actionName](...args);
  } else {
    this.sendAction(actionName,...args);

  },

  actions: {
    enter(info,username) {
      this._actionHandler('sendAction',info,username);

    }
  }

});
```

The purpose of the component is to make it easy for someone to add a chat feature to their application without having to understand the internals of the service that we created earlier. To use this component, the template must be in block or non-block form with these properties:

```
{{sockjs-chat
url='http://localhost:7000'
receiveAction=(action 'receiveMessage')
sendAction=(action 'sendMessage') }}
```

The url property is the location of the WebSocket. The receiveAction method is the parent component's action name. This will be triggered whenever a message is received. The sendAction method is the parent component's name for action that will be sending out messages.

Let's take a look at the component in more detail:

```
layout,
message:'',
init() {
  this._super(...arguments);
  this.get('sockjs').setupSockjs(this.attrs.url);
  this.get('sockjs').on
    ('messageReceived',this,(message)=>{
    this.set('message',message);
    this._actionHandler('receiveAction',message);
  });
},
```

The `layout` property is the same as `layout: layout`. This is a part of ES6. The `init` hook is run when the component is initialized. Whenever you `extend` a built-in method, it's always a good idea to run `this._super`. This makes sure that the component is set up correctly. The `...arguments` array is a part of the new ES6 syntax. It's known as `Rest` parameters and represents an indefinite number of arguments in an array. We'll be using this several times in this component.

After `super` is run, we pass the `url` property to the `setupSockjs` method in our service. The `this.attrs.url` retrieves the `url` property that was passed to the component.

As we are using the `Ember.Event` mixin, we can subscribe to the service and watch for the `messageReceived` trigger. When `messageReceived` is triggered, we set the internal message, `this.message` property, to the message that received. We then pass the message to a new method called `_actionHandler`:

```
_actionHandler(actionName, ...args) {

  if(this.attrs && typeOf
    (this.attrs[actionName]) === 'function'){
    this.attrs[actionName](...args);
  } else {
    this.sendAction(actionName,...args);
  }
},
```

The purpose of `actionHandler` is to take an `action` passed by the `receiveAction` or `sendAction` property and invoke it. However, we need to make sure that we can handle actions passed via closure actions, as described in *Chapter 6, Ember Components*, or just a named action. If it's a closure action such as `(action 'receiveMessage')`, then we simply call it using `this.attrs[actionname](...args)`. If not, then we use `sendAction`, which will send the action to the parent component:

```
actions: {
  enter(info,username) {
    this._actionHandler('sendAction',info,username);

  }
}
```

The `enter` action calls the action handler and passes the `info` and `username` over. As we are using `Rest` parameters in `_actionHandler`, `(...arguments)`, we can pass to it as many arguments as we need.

7. Update the component template for `sockjs-chat.hbs`:

```
// addon/templates/components/sockjs-chat.hbs
{{#if hasBlock}}
    {{yield this}}
{{else}}

    <textarea id="chat-content"
      style="width:500px;height:300px" ></textarea><br/>
    {{input type='text' placeholder='User Name'
      value=uname}}
    {{input type='text' placeholder='Chat Message'
      value=mess}}
    <button {{action 'enter' mess uname}}>Send</button><br>

{{/if}}
```

This gives the user a couple of choices when using this add-on. They can use the component in block form, which will look similar to the service we created in the last chapter, or they can design their own. The `hasBlock` helper returns `true` if the user adds the component in block form. If the component was not added in block form, then it displays the normal chat window.

One important aspect in this template is `{{yield this}}`. When in block form, this will give the block access to the component itself. We'll have full access to the components, properties, and methods in the templates block. We'll take a look at this when we test the add-on.

Testing the sockjs-chat add-on

The /tests folder in the add-on is where all the test cases reside. This is very similar to any other Ember application. However, add-ons also include a dummy folder in the test folder. This folder is generally where add-on makers create their test applications. The program in this folder will have access to the add-on, although you'll need to install any Bower dependencies manually.

1. Run this command to install sockjs-client for testing purposes in the add-on folder:

    ```
    $ bower install sockjs-client --save-dev
    ```

    This will install sockjs-client in the bower.json devDependencies section. The bower.json file is used only for the application in the /tests/dummy/ folder.

2. Update the ember-cli-build.js file with SockJS bower_component:

    ```
    // ember-cli-build.js
    /*jshint node:true*/
    /* global require, module */
    var EmberAddon = require('ember-cli/lib/broccoli/ember-
      addon');

    module.exports = function(defaults) {
        var app = new EmberAddon(defaults, {
          // Add options here
        });

    /*
    This build file specifes the options for the dummy test app of
    this
    addon, located in `/tests/dummy`
    This build file does *not* influence how the addon or the app
    using it
    behave. You most likely want to be modifying `./index.js` or app's
    build file
    */

        app.import('bower_components/sockjs-client/dist/sockjs-
          0.3.4.js');
        return app.toTree();
    };
    ```

    This will add the sockjs-client library to our /tests/dummy app.

3. In the `/tests/dummy` folder, add the component from the add-on in a non-block form:

```
// tests/dummy/app/templates/application.hbs
<h2 id="title">Welcome to Ember</h2>

{{sockjs-chat
url='http://localhost:7000'
receiveAction=(action 'receiveMessage')
sendAction=(action 'sendMessage') }}
```

This will add our new component add-on to the application. The `url` property will be passed to the service so that it can connect to the WebSocket server at port `7000`. The `receiveAction` and `sendAction` properties point to closure actions. This will trigger when we receive a message or want to send a message.

4. Define the send and receive actions in the application controller:

```
// tests/dummy/app/controllers/application.js

import Ember from 'ember';
const {$} = Ember;
export default Ember.Controller.extend({
    sockjs: Ember.inject.service('sockjs'),
    actions:{
      receiveMessage(message){
        $('#chat-content').val((i, text)=>
        `${text}${message}\n`
        );
        this.set('message',message);

      },
      sendMessage(message, username){
        console.log(username);
        console.log(message);
        var send = this.get('sockjs');
        send.sendInfo(`${username}: ${message}`);

      }
    }
});
```

These `actions` handle the sending and receiving of messages. The `receive` method uses a little bit of jQuery to append the latest message to the chat window. The `send` method uses the service from the add-on to send a message.

5. Run `ember server` command and test out the add-on:

   ```
   $ ember server
   ```

   You can run the server command directly in the `add-on` folder. This will serve up the files in the `/tests/dummy/` folder. Make sure to also begin the WebSockets server as well. Check out the last recipe on how to create a WebSocket server in Node.js.

6. Open a web browser and type in a message:

This chat box is generated from the template in the add-on. The message typed here will be sent using the action created in the controller.

7. Use the component in block form and create your own chat box:

```
// tests/dummy/app/templates/application.hbs
<h2 id="title">Welcome to Ember</h2>

{{outlet}}

<h2>Alternative</h2>
{{#sockjs-chat
url='http://localhost:7000'
receiveAction=(action 'receiveMessage')
sendAction=(action 'sendMessage') as |sockjs|}}

    <textarea id="chat-content"
      style="width:300px;height:300px"></textarea><br/>
    {{input type='text' placeholder='User Name' value=uname}}
    {{input type='text' placeholder='Chat Message' value=mess}}
    <button {{action 'enter' mess uname
      target=sockjs}}>Send</button><br>
    {{sockjs.message}}

{{/sockjs-chat}}
```

This template uses the add-on component in block form. This time, we create a smaller chat room instead of using the default one created by the add-on:

```
{{#sockjs-chat
url='http://localhost:7000'
receiveAction=(action 'receiveMessage')
sendAction=(action 'sendMessage') as |sockjs|}}
```

When a component begins with hash #, it's considered to be in block form. To get access to the component itself, we add |sockjs| at the end. Now sockjs has access to all the properties in the component:

```
<button {{action 'enter' mess uname
  target=sockjs}}>Send</button><br>
```

As we have access to the component in the block, we can set target of this action to sockjs. We can also display the message anywhere we need to:

```
    {{sockjs.message}}
```

This will display the message property in the component.

8. Run `ember server` again in the `add-on` folder and open a web browser. Type in a message:

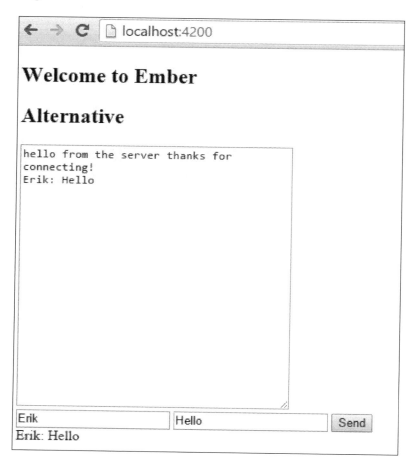

As you can see, this new chat window looks a little different. However, it behaves in the same way and uses the same add-on as before.

9. Create a new application and link it to the add-on to test:

```
$ cd sockjs-chat
$ npm link
$ cd ..
$ ember new chat
$ cd chat
$ npm link sockjs-chat
```

The first thing that we do is navigate to the `sockjs-chat` folder that has our new add-on in it. We then run the `npm link` command. This generates a symbolic link from the local NPM cache to the add-on project. To access the add-on, we must then run `npm link sockjs-chat` in our new application. This creates a link to the add-on.

10. Add the add-on to the `package.json` file in the chat test application:

```
// chat/package.json
...
    "devDependencies": {
    "sockjs-chat": "*"
...
```

This is one of the last steps when linking an add-on to test. Ember must have this code in `devDependencies` for it to see the add-on.

11. Run install and add the blueprint:

```
$ npm install
$ ember g sockjs-chat
```

After updating the `package.json` file, we must install the new package using `npm install`. Finally, running `ember g sockjs-chat` runs the default blueprint that will install `sockjs-client` in the application. The blueprint is automatically run when a new Ember add-on is installed. However, we must run it manually if we use the `npm link` technique.

We can now use the add-on in the application. Take note that we'll need to implement the same controller as we did in the dummy application to make this add-on work.

Publishing the sockjs-chat add-on

There are two ways to publish the new add-on. We can use either NPM or Git.

1. Publish your add-on to a private Git repository:

```
$ cd sockjs-chat
$ git add .
$ git commit -m "first commit"
$ git remote add origin git@yourserver:username/sockjs-chat.git
$ git push origin master
```

To publish privately, you need to set up a private Git repository. Then push the add-on to this repository. In this case, replace `yourserver:username` with the `server` and `username` of your private Git repository.

2. Install the add-on from the Git repository in a new application:

```
$ cd my-app
$ ember install git+ssh://git@yourserver:username/sockjs-chat.git
```

This will install the add-on in the application. Make sure that the name of the repository matches the name of the add-on, or you'll get a message that the add-on cannot be found.

3. Publish your add-on to NPM:

```
$ cd sockjs-chat
$ npm adduser
$ npm publish
```

This will add you as a new user to the `http://npm.org` site. You can then publish the npm as long as the `package.json` file is set up correctly. Later, you can use the npm version to bump the add-on version if needed.

4. Install your add-on in a new application:

```
$ cd my-app2
$ ember install sockjs-chat
```

This will install the `sockjs-chat` application from npm in the `my-app2` application.

How it works...

Ember uses an add-on system to share code between applications. Each add-on has its own package that can be added to any application. Unlike the Bower package manager, these libraries can be more complicated and can encapsulate Ember code.

Ember add-ons can be accessed via NPM or private Git server. This can be used to share information between applications.

See also

Using Ember Addons can really speed up the development process. There are thousands of add-ons available. Check out the following two websites:

- `http://www.emberaddons.com/`
- `http://emberobserver.com/`

Both websites list add-ons and rank them. Use them for your applications. You won't regret it.

Learning the Ember run loop

The Ember `run` loop is an extremely important part of Ember's internals. The `run` loop is used to batch, order, and work in a way that's most efficient for the Ember application. In this recipe, we'll create a simple timer and take a look at how the `run` loop works.

Getting ready

Before we move on to our recipe, we'll need to understand some basics of the Ember `run` loop.

Understanding Ember run queues

The Ember `run` loop consists of six queues as follows:

- `sync`: This queue consists of binding synchronization jobs.
- `actions`: This queue contains general work and promises.
- `routerTransitions`: This queue contains transition jobs in the router.
- `render`: This queue contains jobs meant to render, usually to update the DOM.
- `afterRender`: This queue is run after all previously scheduled render tasks are completed. This queue is typically used for third-party applications.
- `destroy`: This last queue tears down objects.

These queues don't run all the time. They only run in response to certain user and timer events. This way, responsibility is handed back to the user; otherwise, the browser would hang.

When should you change the Ember run loop?

You should make changes to the Ember `run` loop only in certain situations:

- Asynchronous callbacks
- Dealing with timers
- Ajax callbacks
- Certain types of tests
- WebSockets
- `PostMessage` and `messageChannel` event handlers

Most of the time, Ember's `run` loop will handle everything and you won't need to touch it.

Working with the Ember.run namespace

The Ember run namespace gives us several methods to use when working with the `run` loop. The most popular methods are as follows:

▶ `Ember.run.bind`: This is great for use in third-party libraries, and adds the execution of the function to Ember's `run` loop

▶ `Ember.run.later`: This runs the passed target/method after a specified period of time

▶ `Ember.run.schedule`: This runs the passed target/method and optional arguments to the named queue at the end of the loop

There are more methods available, but these are the ones you'll use the most when you need to manipulate the `run` loop.

How to do it...

1. In a new application, generate a new `time-checker` component:

   ```
   $ ember g component time-checker
   $ bower install moment -save
   ```

   This will generate a new component called `time-checker`. In addition, we'll be using the Moment library to keep track of our timer.

2. Import the Moment library to the application:

   ```
   // ember-cli-build.js
   /*jshint node:true*/
   /* global require, module */
   var EmberApp = require('ember-cli/lib/broccoli/ember-app');

   module.exports = function(defaults) {
       var app = new EmberApp(defaults, {
         // Add options here
       });

       app.import('bower_components/moment/min/moment.min.js');

       return app.toTree();
   };
   ```

   This adds the Moment library to the application.

3. Update the new `time-checker.js` component file. Add two properties to it—one to show the time when the component started and another to show the current time:

```js
// app/components/time-checker.js
/* global moment */
import Ember from 'ember';

export default Ember.Component.extend({
    startTime: null,
    currentTime:null,
    init(){
      this._super(...arguments);
      this.set('startTime',moment());
      this.startWatchingTime();

    },
    startWatchingTime(){
      this.set('currentTime', moment());
      Ember.run.later(()=>{
        this.startWatchingTime();
      }, 1000);
    },
    diff: Ember.computed('startTime','currentTime',
      function(){
      return this.get('currentTime').diff
        (this.get('startTime'),'seconds');

    })
});
```

The purpose of this component is to display the time when the component loaded and the current time. It also shows the difference between these two times. Let's take a look at this in more detail:

```js
init(){
    this._super(...arguments);
    this.set('startTime',moment());
    this.startWatchingTime();

},
    startWatchingTime(){
      this.set('currentTime', moment());
      Ember.run.later(()=>{
        this.startWatchingTime();
      }, 1000);
```

The `init` function runs as soon as the component is instantiated. It sets the current time and calls the `startWatchingTime` method. This method uses `Ember.run.later` to wait a second before continuing. Each second, it calls itself, and then calculates the new date and time again. It's better to use this method than `setTimeout`, as it may cause issues in the Ember `run` loop:

```
diff: Ember.computed('startTime','currentTime',
  function(){
  return  this.get('currentTime')
    .diff(this.get('startTime'),'seconds');


})
```

The `diff` computed property updates whenever `currentTime` changes. It returns the difference in seconds between the two times.

4. Update the template for the `time-checker.hbs` component file:

```
// app/templates/components/time-checker.hbs
Startup time: {{startTime}}<br>
Current time: {{currentTime}}<br>
Difference: {{diff}}
```

This will display the start, current, and difference times.

5. Update the application template and add the component:

```
<h2 id="title">Welcome to Ember</h2>

{{time-checker}}
```

This will add the `time-checker` component to the application.

6. Run the application and you'll see two times. The second time will update every second:

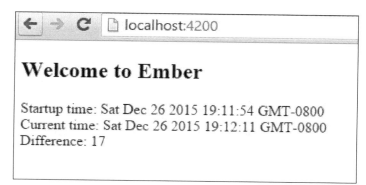

The Ember `run` loop makes this possible.

How it works...

The Ember `run` loop helps schedule work in an Ember application. It runs whenever there is user action or certain timing events. It consists of six different queues. Each queue is responsible for different functions in the application.

In most situations, you don't need to worry about the `run` loop. However, in some situations such as dealing with asynchronous callbacks or timing events, you'll need to use them. Keep this in mind as you continue to program in the future.

Index

Thank you for buying
Ember.js Cookbook

About Packt Publishing

Packt, pronounced 'packed', published its first book, *Mastering phpMyAdmin for Effective MySQL Management*, in April 2004, and subsequently continued to specialize in publishing highly focused books on specific technologies and solutions.

Our books and publications share the experiences of your fellow IT professionals in adapting and customizing today's systems, applications, and frameworks. Our solution-based books give you the knowledge and power to customize the software and technologies you're using to get the job done. Packt books are more specific and less general than the IT books you have seen in the past. Our unique business model allows us to bring you more focused information, giving you more of what you need to know, and less of what you don't.

Packt is a modern yet unique publishing company that focuses on producing quality, cutting-edge books for communities of developers, administrators, and newbies alike. For more information, please visit our website at www.packtpub.com.

About Packt Open Source

In 2010, Packt launched two new brands, Packt Open Source and Packt Enterprise, in order to continue its focus on specialization. This book is part of the Packt open source brand, home to books published on software built around open source licenses, and offering information to anybody from advanced developers to budding web designers. The Open Source brand also runs Packt's open source Royalty Scheme, by which Packt gives a royalty to each open source project about whose software a book is sold.

Writing for Packt

We welcome all inquiries from people who are interested in authoring. Book proposals should be sent to author@packtpub.com. If your book idea is still at an early stage and you would like to discuss it first before writing a formal book proposal, then please contact us; one of our commissioning editors will get in touch with you.

We're not just looking for published authors; if you have strong technical skills but no writing experience, our experienced editors can help you develop a writing career, or simply get some additional reward for your expertise.

open source _{community experience distilled}

Mastering Ember.js

ISBN: 978-1-78398-198-4   Paperback: 218 pages

Build fast, scalable, dynamic, and ambitious single-page web applications by mastering Ember.js

1. Create, test, and deploy powerful and professional web applications.

2. Debug and modularize your project effectively.

3. Easily architect solutions to any single page web application needs.

Rapid Ember.js [Video]

ISBN: 978-1-78439-765-4   Durations: 00:60 hours

Build dynamic and data-driven web applications from the ground up using Ember.js.

1. Build nested and detailed application structures easily with Ember's router.

2. Enrich your web applications with Ember's powerful data-bound features.

3. Update your web page content and styles based on the underlying data automatically.

Please check **www.PacktPub.com** for information on our titles

Ember.js Web Development
with Ember CLI

Build ambitious single-page web applications using the power of
Ember.js and Ember CLI

Suchit Puri

Ember.js Web Development with Ember CLI

ISBN: 978-1-78439-584-1   Paperback: 174 pages

Build ambitious single-page web applications using the power of Ember.js and Ember CLI

1. Build scalable web applications with Ember.js and Ember CLI

2. Leverage the working examples to gain more insight into the Ember framework

3. Manage dependencies and use the broccoli asset pipeline, the ES6 compatible module system, and more with a strong Ember CLI focus

INSTANT
Short | Fast | Focused

Ember.js Application
Development How-to

Your first step in creating amazing web applications

Marc Bodmer

Instant Ember.js Application Development How-to

ISBN: 978-1-78216-338-1   Paperback: 48 pages

Your first step in creating amazing web applications

1. Learn something new in an Instant! A short, fast, focused guide delivering immediate results.

2. Create semantic HTML templates using Handlebars.

3. Lay the foundation for large web applications using the latest version of Ember.js in an easy to follow format.

Please check **www.PacktPub.com** for information on our titles

Made in the USA
Middletown, DE
23 January 2018